Praise for *Rou*

"A powerful story of resilience and grit, Pascual's story is an instant community gem centered on overcoming trauma and maintaining hope. This book proves to be on the right T.R.A.A.C.K. as a resource for teachers and students alike!"

—Dr. Juan A. Baez, Principal, Milwaukee Public Schools

"A story of adversity and challenge as well as resilience and success. Though Pascual safely "makes it home," not all in his situation would. His poignant story is a call to action for educators - novice and veteran - to ensure all students not only survive but THRIVE.

—Christin Johnson, School Counselor

"Through the eyes of an educator who has persevered through life with a high ACE score, we learn how to instill hope and help students rise, achieve, and succeed in spite of exposure to past and present traumas. This is a must-read for any educator who wants to learn how to build relationships with students and change the course of a student's life for the better."

– Rebecca Reyes-Clement, Elementary Special Education Teacher

"Pascual Rodriguez provides a thoughtful and powerful framework for educators and future educators to approach connecting with and supporting the children they work with. He interweaves unforgettable accounts of his own remarkable experience (both as a child and an educator) with psychology and theory. The reader ends the book with much to reflect about in relation to how they approach students and concrete takeaways for fostering their students' growth and maturation as people.

– Dr. Gabriel Velez, Asst. Professor and Developmental Psychologist

Rounding Third and Finally Home:

An Educator's Life Journey of Triumph Over Failure

Other books by or with Judith Gwinn Adrian:

A Purpose-Driven Life of Helping Others
(2022) HenschelHAUS
Written with Diane Pauly

Walking the Line: There is No Room for Hate
(2022)HenschelHAUS
Written with Joshua Clauer

Nancer the Dancer: Myositis and Me
(2020) HenschelHAUS
Reader's Choice – five stars

Tera's Tale: Rebel on the River
(2019)HenschelHAUS
Finalist, Eric Hoffer/Montaigne Medal

In Warm Blood: Prison & Privilege, Hurt & Heart
Written with DarRen Morris
(2015) HenschelHAUS
Finalist, USA Book Awards: 2015
non-fiction Multi-cultural and True Crime categories

Because I Am Jackie Millar
written with Jackie Millar
(2007 & 2010) Golden The Press

ROUNDING THIRD AND FINALLY HOME:

An Educator's Life Journey of Triumph Over Failure

Pascual Rodriguez
with
Judith Gwinn Adrian

Henschel
HAUS
publishing, inc.
Milwaukee, Wisconsin

Published by HenschelHAUS Publishing, Inc.
Milwaukee, Wisconsin
www.henschelHAUSbooks.com

Please contact the publisher for quantity discounts.

ISBN: 978159598-921-5
E-ISBN: 978159598-922-2
LCCN: 2022943587

Cover design by Edwin Robles, Art Director

TABLE OF CONTENTS

DEDICATION

Not a day goes by where the memories of my parents—in particular my mother—fail to occupy my heart, mind, and soul. It's been 12 years since her passing and the pain is just as poignant today. However, her presence continues to manifest throughout my day, warming my heart, knowing she is with me with every breath I take.

Although many individuals have contributed to my life, career, and successes, I dedicate this book in her memory for showing me the true meaning of perseverance, love, and forgiveness.

Maria Rodriguez—Mami—was born on April 16, 1939, in the city of Cayey, Puerto Rico. She remained there until she migrated to the United States during the late 1950s. Throughout this book, I divulge stories of the good, the bad, and the beautiful. As you read, you will be drawn into moments of well-being, imagery of distressing incidents, and the silver lining of hope—all in many ways involving my mother.

Through all these moments, Mami persevered, reconnected with her love for her children and grandchildren, and continued her faith in God's forgiving heart. Our family was blessed to have her with us on earth for 71 years. I honor her life, her love, and her continuous presence in our lives through this memoir. I love you, Mami.

FOREWORD

Pascual and I grew up in what are now known as Milwaukee's Riverwest and Brewers Hill neighborhoods, poorer neighborhoods back then, where many Puerto Ricans lived filled with cultural pride. Pascual and I were mere acquaintances at that time. It wasn't until our paths crossed again professionally at the United Community Center (UCC) that our relationship began.

UCC, a larger community-based organization serving primarily Hispanics on the near south side of Milwaukee, offered an array of programs. Pascual was the principal of the school and I was the Director of Marketing and Public Relations. During the many administrative meetings that we attended together, committees and events, I was frequently and pleasantly surprised by his no-nonsense demeanor. He wasn't there to impress anyone. He wasn't there for status or power. His mission was well known: the well-being of his students. I admired how children ran to him and wrapped their arms around his legs and how he embraced them with genuine affection.

Our relationship turned from professional to friendship when Pascual and his family began to attend the church I attended. Their love of family, of community, and of each other drew me in and filled my life in so many beautiful and unexpected ways.

Over time, I began to learn about Pascual's life—about his survival. When you begin reading this book, you might feel horror, anger, pity, and compassion, as I did. You'll learn about the unthinkable abuse and neglect he suffered for many years both in his home and in the school system. You'll learn how he survived on intermittent acts of kindness.

Pascual has fittingly used baseball analogies throughout his book. Baseball was a lifeline that opened his world to new possibilities. In baseball, it was about what he brought to the table. It gave him confidence, hope, and power. It helped him to understand his WHY and his purpose.

It's difficult to understand how trauma can ruin some lives, yet others are able to use it as their foundation for growth. Pascual chose the latter. Despite the tragedy and trauma, this book is really about survival, perseverance, hope, faith, and even forgiveness.

I'm neither a writer nor an expert in trauma, therefore I was both humbled and honored that Pascual asked me to write the foreword to his book. While we share the same cultural background, grew up in the same neighborhood, share a strong work ethic, moral principles, and family values, I think it was his witness to my five-year battle with cancer that moved him to ask. We've chosen not to allow our difficulties to define who we are.

Pascual has taken it further. Not only did he decide that his past wouldn't define his future, he became an educator and a principal. He made it his mission to personally touch the lives of kids who, like him, were falling through the cracks, failed by the system. He then decided that there's more to do and he embarked on a journey to create exponential change. He created an intervention blueprint, T.R.A.A.C.K. to Impact. His innovative blueprint, developed for educators, addresses six universal traits to ensure students' social and emotional well-being. "We need to see children as people/human before we treat them as students."

If you are an educator, a parent or a caring adult; if you are a youth in trouble, you'll find this book life changing.

—Luz Ortiz-Carby, retired Administrator

PREFACE

Dreams may be shredded but hope always prevails!

As early as I can remember, the dream of becoming a professional baseball player permeated my soul. From the first moment my parents and I entered the hallowed grounds of County Stadium, where the Milwaukee Brewers played, I was obsessed with America's pastime. The smell of freshly cut grass, the aroma of hotdogs and brats, the cool icy taste of a soft drink, and that magical crack of a bat, drew me in hook, line, and sinker. The sight of early arriving baseball fanatics standing in the bleacher sections during batting practice, eagerly holding out their gloves in anticipation of baseballs flying their way, added to the excitement. I was hooked. I was experiencing the emotional connection of first love, a feeling I did not experience again until I began dating Caroline, my future wife.

My dream of playing baseball was clearly deep-seated. It was an ambitious dream but one I was willing to work for. Unfortunately, over the next decade and a half, I was not afforded opportunities to play even Little League baseball. Still, I found myself in the proverbial batter's box as life threw nothing but curveballs in my direction.

There were many swings and misses as I had to learn how to adjust to my world. Baseball serves as the perfect analogy for my journey from the batter's box, around first, second, and third bases until finally reaching home.

For years, my "busyness" with school, work, and family served as a blanket of emotional protection. But eventually, the traumas from those early swings and misses began to surface. The blanket was lifted. I used to think about how life could have been different. Ultimately, I came to the realization that my experiences, some more difficult to bear than others, have shaped me into the person I am today. I made a conscious decision to survive and thrive. I learned that I could not always control what was happening. But life goes on, and although we forgive, we always remember.

Why am I writing this book? For whom?

Those are two questions I asked myself before embarking on this venture. I certainly hope that, after reading this book, it will become as clear to you, as it has for me, the answer to my *why*, and perhaps some clues to your *why* as well. As you read through each of the "Innings," my hope is to provide you with a context that begins with the early years of our family's household experience. I invite you to travel with me as I allow vulnerability to guide us through my childhood journey, culminating in a "how to" platform used to guide readers, educators, business owners, and leaders from all professions to a humbled response to those who have experienced trauma in their lives.

The word *why* is not used from the context of why things happened but rather from a connotative perspective of *why* I exist in this world and what is the purpose behind my *why*. As John Maxwell puts it, "When I discover my why, my purpose, and start moving towards it, I soon discover my *wow!*" (Maxwell, 2013).

In addition, Simon Sinek's premise in his book, *Start with Why*, is "People don't buy what you do, they buy why you do it." Sinek also states, "We imagine a world in which the vast majority of people wake up every day inspired, feel safe wherever they are, and end the day fulfilled by the work they do."

PREFACE

Does your *why* give you the fulfillment and understanding that what you did today was what was needed to make the lives of others better today than yesterday and positioned to be better tomorrow than today? This concept required me to do some deep self reflection, which led me down an inquisitive journey: *How did I learn from my life experiences? What have I learned? What did I do with that learning? How did others benefit from that learning?*

Emerging from both my early life experiences and my work as an educator, I have developed a new way of teaching that is attuned to the social and emotional well-being of our students (and employees). It is called **T.R.A.A.C.K. to IMPACT**, a concept I will elaborate on further in the 9th Inning (chapter).

First, however, I will take you through my life's ups and downs: happy moments, sad moments, and dark moments, to set the context for the development of T.R.A.A.C.K. to IMPACT. In addition, I have included at the end of each inning (chapter), a "Reflection" section to provide a space where you can connect your own life's experiences with what was read, asking how these experiences have shaped your life.

Subsequently, all of this work revealed to me that hope is the ray of light we all must discover, even in our darkest moments, to navigate us to a place where we can use our wisdom to serve and help others running around the bases of their diamond of life and experiencing their *wow*, while ultimately finding their own personal *home*.

ON DECK—
MY "WHY" REVEALED

The two most important days of your life
are the day you were born and the day you find out why.
—Mark Twain

*N*o. A single word. A mere syllable. And yet this seemingly simple word changed the course of my life more than once. That word not only constructed who I am today, but equally importantly, revealed my *why*.

As a child, I dreamed of playing professional baseball. I was not unique in this dream. I wanted to be one of those impoverished kids who overcame the statistical odds by realizing his dreams through sports and using them to find my way out of the Hood.

My Hood was the Riverwest Latino community in Milwaukee, Wisconsin. Not far away, bats cracked and fans cheered as the Milwaukee Brewers practiced and played. And as a boy, I idolized players like George Brett, Graig Nettles, and Milwaukee's own Sixto Lezcano.

My father took my mom and me to County Stadium (later Miller Park and now American Family Field), home of the Braves —and subsequently the Brewers. We would sit in the right field bleachers, where I remember Hank Aaron and later Sixto were positioned during games. Why right field? Because of the star

5

power that occupied that side of the field. Sitting near the dugout and imagining being a player strengthened my dream. It didn't matter that the bleacher seats were the cheaper seats. What mattered was I was in the presence of greatness.

The bleachers were known as the party section where most people drank and had a good time. Compared to the grandstands, the bleachers were basic rows of benches, offering no comfort. In contrast, the grandstands included individual chair-back seats, which limited your ability to move around. When attendance was low, I would run up and down the bleachers, frequently stopping next to the bullpen to watch the Brewers' relief pitchers. Channeling my deepest and loudest man-child voice, I attempted to shout over the roar of cheering fans, "Hey, mister, can I have a ball?" Occasionally getting their attention, and to my surprise and delight, someone would toss a ball my way. It was AWESOME!

We didn't have much as a family, but life seemed normal. Most everyone around us lived in the same manner. How could I know that we were economically poor? We were rich in family and that was all that mattered.

I was never afforded the opportunity to play Little League baseball or any organized baseball, outside of strike-out, which is a form of baseball utilizing a wall as your backstop, pitcher, and batter. In our household, there wasn't much family support for Little League baseball, or for that matter, any form of sports activities outside of fishing.

Be that as it may, nine years later my dream of becoming a professional baseball player was reborn. Once again, it was an ambitious dream and one I was willing to sacrifice just about anything to achieve.

I was 19 years old and had no clue what my future plans were. I knew I had a dream and time was running out. It was while attending a Brewer's game with my then-girlfriend,

Caroline, that I discovered my "aha" moment. It was the first game I had attended since I was a child.

During the excitement of the game I caught a foul ball—a chance opportunity. I asked myself, *Is this a sign that I should rekindle my dream of playing professionally?* I do believe signs help us in certain situations or when faced with challenges.

Full of excitement and emotion, I stared at the green grass, the infield, and the players. I realized that, with no background or experience of officially playing the game, my dream was fading fast.

I made a bold decision to work toward the nearly impossible task of pursuing that dream. For the next two years, I dedicated a minimum of eight hours a day, five to six days a week, to practicing and working out. My baseball home was anywhere I could throw a ball, run, and swing a bat.

Eventually, I found a league that would provide the *Field of Dreams* I sought to hone my skills. I volunteered my services to the local Felix Mantilla Little League organization run by the United Community Center (UCC). This Center provided programs to Hispanics and other Milwaukee residents. I volunteered in hopes of helping younger players boost their chances of achieving their baseball dreams, big or small, as well as perfecting my own skills. In fact, the Center still provides programs and now has two charter schools under its umbrella—Bruce Guadalupe Community School (BGCS) and Acosta Middle School. I was later privileged to serve as principal at BGCS for nineteen years.

In the fall of 1989, my cousin, two friends, and I moved to Puerto Rico. We all had hopes of trying out with several Major League baseball organizations. It was a long shot but what did we have to lose? We were granted our first opportunity for try-outs with the California Angels. Vic Power, a former Minnesota

Twins major league player, put us through rigorous try-out exercises. Typically, players are evaluated on a scale of one-to-five, with five being the highest score possible.

These scores were evaluated in four different categories:

- Running (speed),
- Fielding,
- Throwing, and
- Hitting.

After completing the try-out, I was informed that I had been given a high rating on three of the four categories, with throwing being the lowest score. Naturally, I was thrilled and excited. I couldn't help but think to myself, *Could this be the team? My team?*

Shortly thereafter, I received a phone call from none other than Vic Power offering me a minor league contract. The investment in hours of sacrifice, sweat, and hard work was finally paying off. My dream was beginning to unfold. Soon I would be considered a professional baseball player. I was on my way.

After consulting with Felix Ramos—the man who had been coaching me in Milwaukee—regarding the details of the contract, I was advised to reject the first offer. Major league organizations were known to low-ball players.

My coach was correct. The California Angels offered a $1000 signing bonus. Did I reject it and go to the negotiating table? Absolutely not! Without any hesitation, I went against my coach's advice and immediately accepted the offer.

As one can imagine, my coach was not happy. However, for me, it wasn't about the money. It was about fulfilling the dream that I thought was virtually impossible to attain. In my heart, I could not justify rejecting that offer and jeopardizing a golden opportunity.

Ironically, another fellow was offered the same signing bonus they offered me. He rejected it and ended up being offered a $15,000 signing bonus. As fate would have it, he would soon become my roommate. I was forced to hear that story repeatedly. 20/20 hindsight?

No regrets.

In 1990, I attended spring training with the California Angels. My dream was unfolding. Staring into the mirror, dressed in my uniform for the first time, I was overcome with emotion and unable to stop the tears streaming down my cheeks. Outside of marrying Caroline years later and the birth of our four children, that minute in front of the mirror was the most significant moment in my life. My dream had finally come true.

Unfortunately, that dream dwindled rather quickly. Within the first week of training, I sustained two significant injuries that put me on the disabled list (DL) for a week. Immediately after getting off the DL, I hurt my right knee, which prevented me from running, a skill I excelled at.

Minor League while I was with the California Angels. Injury to right knee ended my professional baseball career. (1990)

This knee injury was devastating to my morale. I was emotionally distraught as I limped into the club house alone. I asked myself, *Why?*

Little did I know that my *why* would shortly be revealed to me.

Several weeks later, as I sat at the trainer's table receiving treatment on my knee, the trainer said, "Coach would like to see you in his office." Given that other players had experienced the same request and were no longer with the team, I feared the worst.

As expected, my coach informed me I was being released. I was only two months into my professional career. I sensed the coach felt badly about delivering this devastating news. He knew my strong work ethic, he saw how dedicated and committed I was to the game. He had tried in vain to keep me on the team. However, it was not his decision. In the end, due to my injuries, he was forced to release me.

He asked if I had anything to say. As he was speaking, I sat in a slouched position as the initial shock of hearing the word *released* hit me like a lightning bolt. As ironic as it may seem, that shock quickly turned into joy. Images of working with youth at St Patrick's church drowned out his words, and I smiled. He again asked, "Do you have anything to say?"

My response was, "No." I had nothing to say.

In that brief moment, my *why* began to unfold. It was that second important day: *The two most important days of your life are the day you were born and the day you find out why.* The countless hours of training had not been in vain. My *why* would reveal what I had actually been in training for the previous nine years and would continue for the next thirty-plus years of my life.

Reflections

- Are you living your *why*?

- Are others benefiting from your *why*?

- How can you use your *why* for positive change in your community and/or work environment?

My son, Pascual Jr., and me meeting Hank Aaron.

1990 Minor League picture.

11

From L to R: Pascual, Mami (Maria), Dalila (sister), Papi (biological father), Alicia (sister) at Dalila's graduation (1988).

INNING 2

HOME-FIELD ADVANTAGE

A home-field advantage. Yes, that is what I was born with. And why not embrace that which is so freely given to you?

My first language was Spanish, so needless to say, my English skills were in continual development. My sisters and I predominantly spoke Spanish at home. It would be years before I would fully appreciate what a valuable gift that was. It was a gift our parents had given us to ensure that our Puerto Rican cultural roots and connections remained strong, which they have.

I delighted in my boyish instinct for annoying the hell out of my two sisters. I'd smile when Mami held out her hands invitingly, and said to me, "*Vente con Mami.* Come to Mommy."

As I hopped toward her, I couldn't resist the urge to smile in pure pleasure as I made my way past my sisters and into Mami's waiting arms. They would glare at me, which only widened my big smile, knowing all the while I was getting under their skin.

I was Mami's favorite (at least in my opinion). I was her youngest child, her baby, and her only boy. When I was born, my uncle said, "*Que pocholito.*" (*Pocholitio* is a Spanish term for being a cute baby.) That name would stick with me. Everyone referred to me as *Pocholo*; no one in the family has ever, in my memory, called me by my given name, Pascual.

I must admit, I was spoiled. Treated like a king by Mami.

I often sat on her lap as she either massaged my back or caressed my hair, showering me with kisses.

As strange as it sounds, one of our favorite pastimes was taking grains of sugar and putting them in my hair. Sugar contains a natural moisturizer that leaves the hair shiny. Mami would pop the grains of sugar onto my scalp with her fingernails. This form of scalp massage was extremely relaxing. I would eventually doze off for twenty or thirty minutes. (I've tried to get my wife, Caroline, to do this, but she refuses!)

As a child, if I wanted to eat something different from what was being served, without hesitation, Mami would make it for me. I have always loved rice and would be content to eat it every day if allowed to do so. When soup was on the dinner menu, I kicked the stove in protest. Mami never made a big deal of my tirade; she simply made a pot of rice or whatever I requested. My sisters, on the other hand, had to eat what was served. End of story.

This special treatment drove my sisters nuts. However, it did not come without consequences and my sisters eventually got their revenge. They enjoyed playing dress up, which included coaxing me into trying on their dresses and shoes. They polished my nails and added Mami's wigs to complete the outfits. Good thing there was no social media at that time, as they would have surely shared that experience with the world.

I don't remember being required to do household chores. I never washed dishes or picked up a broom or mop to clean the floors. My sisters did it all. Papi spent his time fixing his cars or doing minor things around the house. I watched him with fascination, eagerly waiting for him to ask me to pass whatever tools he needed. He was a do-it-yourself kind of dad. Therefore, repairmen were never called. If something needed fixing, Papi would take care of it. I feel fortunate to have inherited those same traits.

Caroline and I have two sons and two daughters. It was important to us both that our children knew and understood that our family worked together. Caroline did not want our girls to grow up thinking they had the responsibility to do the lion's share of the chores. She instilled the belief that they did not have to do everything for a man or that they even had to have a man in their lives. Her philosophy to them was, *I want you to have a man in your life because you want him in your life, not because you need him in your life.* In addition, we raised our boys to share in the household chores. Because of this, our children have adopted the egalitarian philosophy of home life. Our sons love to cook and have become quite skillful in the kitchen.

I see the generational culture shift.

As tradition would have it, Mami continued to take pleasure in serving me dinner, whether my family visited her home or during family gatherings at my sisters' homes. While Mami piled food on my plate, everyone else was left to fend for themselves.

Caroline would laughingly shake her head at this personal service. My thought was always, *Why would I deny Mami that pleasure?*

* * *

While I was growing up, our neighborhood consisted of primarily Puerto Ricans and a few African American and Caucasian families. We lived in a closely-knit neighborhood. My grandparents, aunts, uncles, and cousins lived either next door, across the street, or within walking distance from our home. It was a blessing to have our loved ones close in proximity, sharing and bonding in both good and bad times.

It was not uncommon for family members and neighbors to watch each other's children. Parents felt safe occasionally allowing their children to stay home alone, something almost unheard of these days. Everyone knew one another. If you needed help, the community was there to support and help out any way they could. You know the saying, *It takes a village to raise a child?* My Milwaukee neighborhood was my village.

There was never a lack of food on my block. Somebody was always cooking. It seemed that as soon as breakfast was done, lunch prep began. This was then followed by dinner. Playing outdoors, the smell of *arroz con pollo* (chicken and rice), *bistec* (steak), *lechon* (pork roast) and other delicious Puerto Rican cuisines filled the air, making our stomachs churn with hunger. I can still smell the delicious aromas. We kids would travel from house to house, eating and filling our little bellies throughout the day. This pattern meant more food, more energy, and at times, more opportunities to get ourselves into a little trouble.

If you were caught misbehaving, neighbors wouldn't hesitate to clock you in the head with their knuckles (this was known as a *cocotazo*) and word traveled fast. Soon after you arrived home, your parents would give you another *cocotazo* (this explains all the knots in my head...I received my fair share over the years).

Most weekends, someone on the block was throwing a party. Many times, it was to celebrate a birthday, holiday, or just simply to gather with family and friends. I fondly remember the joyful Christmas parties. The adults would buy gifts—small toys—for every child. The economy was good and everyone seemed to be working. After opening gifts, we kids would head outdoors to play in the yard while the adults inside were having their *coquito* (coconut and rum eggnog).

A traditional family activity was making *pasteles* (somewhat similar to tamales) for the holiday season. It was a yearly tradition that took hours to complete. It was then that family members were able to catch up on the latest gossip and neighborhood happenings. One can anecdotally argue that making the *masa* (dough), which involved grating the green bananas, took roughly 80% of the time.

Our family, in all its uniqueness, would find its inventive spirit in moments of necessity. An example of this was the time our Uncle Mendin was helping make *pasteles*. In a moment of frustration over the time it took to grate the plantains, he decided to invoke that inventive spirit by creating a wooden box and attaching a small motor with a shaft to it. He perforated a bean can, so pointed ridges stuck out. He then poured cement into the can, and manufactured a hole in the box, attaching the can to the motor. The machine was noisy, admittedly, but what had taken hours of work now took fifteen or twenty minutes. Little did we know he had created a food processor. Unfortunately, no one thought about patenting the device. Everyone involved in this tedious process was elated with the creativity that streamlined making the *masa*. Necessity is the mother of invention, but it's

Pastele machine created in 1970 to reduce the time needed to grate plantains from hours to minutes.

also the mother of survival. We lived as a community. We survived as a community.

* * *

Neighborhood life consisted of adults coming home from work and eating dinner, followed by drinking their favorite alcoholic beverage either around the dinner table or on the porch. My parents often visited the neighborhood bars and took me along with them (which was and is legal in Wisconsin). While my parents socialized, I passed the time shooting pool.

I have to say, however, that alcoholism was rampant in the community. My family was no exception. In this seemingly idyllic community, alcohol-induced violence was present within and between families.

I was about six years old when we lived next door to the neighborhood *bodega,* grocery store. The *bodega* was a gathering place in the summer. The neighborhood men bought their beer and sat outside, talking and gambling. (Someone was always watching for the cops.) The store owner, Papo, would occasionally step out and have a beer with his customers while we kids amused ourselves nearby.

Papo played a pennies and candy dice game with the neighborhood kids. If we won, he would give us candy. When we lost, he would take our pennies, although I think he always gave away more candy than he took back in pennies.

One particular day, while playing the dice game with Papo, a neighborhood man named Carlos walked into the store, intoxicated.

Shortly thereafter, Victor also entered the store. Victor had recently suffered a stroke, which had left him with a left-side deficit. Without warning, they began arguing about some money Victor owed Carlos.

Papo remarked in Spanish, "You guys need to take this outside." The situation escalated quickly when Carlos reached into his rear pants pocket, pulled out a knife, and stabbed Victor in the chest. Papo jumped over the counter and pushed me away as he tackled Carlos to the ground.

Fearful and shocked, I began back-pedaling from the entrance of the store and into a parked car that luckily stopped me from going into the busy street.

Mami was sitting on our porch next door, which gave her a clear path to see the look on my face. She made a direct beeline toward me and, in a frantic voice, asked, "*¿Que pasa?* What is going on?" Unable to utter a word, I simply pointed to the bodega as tears welled up in my eyes. Mami quickly helped Papo cover the stab wound with towels to stop the bleeding until the paramedics arrived.

Thankfully, Victor survived the stabbing. However, Carlos did not escape the legal ramifications of his actions. As he sat nearby on the stoop of his home, drunk and with the knife still in hand, the police arrived and took him away. That was the last time we ever saw him.

Needless to say, it was a traumatic experience. But, children are extremely resilient and I was no exception. I managed to bury it, as one of the many terrifying experiences to come, into my subconscious mind.

* * *

My father worked full-time doing die-casting in a factory. In addition to his income, we received supplemental government assistance: monthly living-wage checks and food stamps. Mami, along with some family members, picked crops at Wally's farm in the summer months. They were then laid off after the growing season, which qualified them for assistance.

My cousins and I also worked at Wally's farm in the summer. Wally paid the kids a rate of $1 an hour. (I don't know what he paid the adults). The labor consisted of picking dried beans and digging up potatoes.

Digging up potatoes was one of the most painstaking jobs, due to the mice we would occasionally spot, which left me constantly on the look-out, afraid I would see one. This was no different than at home where we had an infestation of rodents. One night, while sleeping, a rat climbed on my parent's bed and onto Mami's chest. The pressure of the rat woke her up. In a natural reaction, Mami attempted to push the rat off her chest, resulting in the rat instinctively biting her finger. This may explain my fear of mice, even the little cute ones.

In addition to mice, I detested farm work because it was physically grueling, not to mention having to work in summer temperatures, which were typically hot. Working in the scorching heat, I couldn't help but think, *I wish I was home.*

When it came to picking beans, it seemed like the bushel basket would never fill up as if it was a bottomless pit. There was no concept of time carrying out this laborious work, whether I was picking beans or digging potatoes. No matter how fast I picked, it always seemed like a half-full bushel was staring at me. When Mami would occasionally eat a bean or two, confused, I would think, *Who would want to voluntarily eat that?* There is not much incentive to snack on vegetables especially when you've been picking them for hours.

* * *

While Papi went to work, as most of the men in our neighborhood did, Mami stayed home much of the year. After school, we routinely had dinner as a family. Papi undoubtedly received a heaping amount. It was an unspoken belief that the man of the house received the biggest portion of food. Papi may have been the king of the home, but Mami frequently had the last word. Nonetheless, like any relationship, they had their share of arguments.

We always had food on the table and clothes on our backs. From that standpoint, Papi supported his family. I can surely attest that there was nothing but pure love at our family table in the early years. Love, but not perfection.

In the midst of that love, like typical siblings, my sisters annoyed each other and argued quite often. I'm sure I didn't help.

My eldest sister, Alicia, had a different relationship with Mami than I did. More strained. Their relationship was tested and inevitably reached a breaking point.

One day, Alicia returned home from Lincoln High School and Mami happened to be in an unfavorable and irritable mood. Like most young ladies entering their high school teenage years, my sister wanted to fit in with her peers, so wearing a little make-up wasn't out of the ordinary, at least away from home.

As Alicia entered the house, she attempted to hurriedly sneak past Mami to reach her room on the far end of the attic. However, Mami, without missing a beat, noticed the make-up and followed Alicia up the stairs. She pushed the bedroom door wide open, and in a fit of rage, began to call Alicia names in Spanish that are (for lack of a better term) associated with prostitutes.

In a swift movement, Mami grabbed Alicia by her long, dark hair and set into motion what could only be described as a major beating (yes, it's a harsh word, but that's what it was). My sister, Dalila, and I sat on the couch downstairs, frozen in fear. Hands over our ears could not cover up the screaming, yelling, and sounds of flying objects, while our poor sister begged for mercy.

It was an impassioned and mournful moment for us that left an indelible mark on our young lives.

Word of the beating traveled fast throughout our family, and before we knew it, Mami Amelia, our grandmother, came and took Alicia away. I'm not sure if my sister wanted to go. Nevertheless, I don't think she had a choice. In my grandmother's eyes, she had the right to remove Alicia from our home, and she was not to be questioned. End of conversation. From then on, Alicia lived with our grandmother, a block away, and did not return home again other than for brief visits.

For some strange reason, Mami took a lot of her frustrations out on Alicia. In retrospect, she seemed envious of our sister's endeavors. Mami, I learned many years later, had been forced to leave behind her dream of becoming a nurse when she left Puerto Rico to move to Milwaukee. Alicia became the first in our family to go to college and graduate, as far as I know. She was very scholarly and dedicated to her studies. She eventually became a nurse, something that filled Mami with both pride and perhaps some envy.

Dalila and I remained with Mami and Papi, adjusting as best as we could. Without a doubt, Dalila was Papi's favorite child. Just as much as I was spoiled by Mami, Dalila was equally spoiled by Papi. As she swept the floor, Papi would intentionally throw crumpled dollar bills on the floor and say, "*Mira, recoge esa basura.* Look, pick up that garbage." She would smile and continue sweeping, making more money in ten minutes sweeping than I did picking beans for several hours at the farm.

In addition, Papi also loved Dalila because she was the family tattletale. He could count on getting all the family gossip and news of the day from her. This behavior, unfortunately, would one day have a significant impact on our family. It was this unintentional behavior that would be the beginning of us losing our home-field advantage!

Reflections

- Why do you think family bonds can remain strong in spite of shared trauma?

- Was there an opportunity, early in life, to learn that choices, not circumstances, determine destiny? In what ways?

Mami and me sharing a moment at my niece's wedding in 2004.

First-grade picture, Oliver Wendell Holmes Elementary School (MPS).

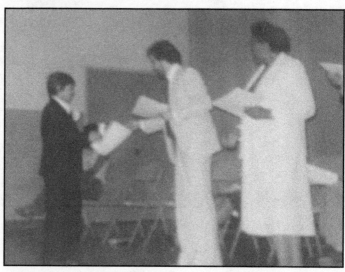

Fifth-grade graduation ceremony, Henry L. Palmer Elementary school (MPS).

INNING 3

HIT BUT COULDN'T RUN

During my elementary school years, I attended Oliver Wendell Holmes, Cass Street School, and Henry L. Palmer School. They were within a mile or less from the many homes we lived in at one point or another. Since we moved a lot, we had to change schools regularly.

True elementary school story: I learned my colors and numbers at an early age from Mami's food stamps.

> $1.00 = Brown stamp
> $5.00 = Purple stamp
> $10.00 = Green stamp

When my K4 teacher introduced these colors to the class, I emphatically said, from the depth of my innocence and in a proud voice, "Those are the colors of my mom's money." The teacher looked at me speechless. It was years later when I understood the teacher's smirk, as if she were holding in her laughter.

Being dependent on government assistance seemed normal. We didn't have much. On the other hand, I didn't know what being rich or being impoverished meant. This all seemed normal, and in my eyes, everyone lived like we did. Life was good, and colorful, I guess.

The numbers and colors were reinforced because Mami would frequently send me to the *bodega* to buy something using food stamps. I would excitedly pull out the pack of colored money from my pocket as if I were rolling in dough.

When we didn't have money on hand, we used *fiao* at the *bodega*. *Fiao* was the credit tab Papo set up for local families, which is a common transaction in many Latino communities. His *bodega* was in an impoverished neighborhood and he understood the economics of this. He allowed families to purchase food, drinks, and home supplies on credit and then pay for them on the first of each month when the welfare checks came in. He kept a large ledger where he documented each purchase.

Having caught on to the concept of purchasing something now and paying for it later, Dalila and I devised a plan that we thought at the time was a brilliant idea. However, it did not end well. We went to the *bodega* and convinced Papo that Mami had given us permission to charge candy on *fiao*. I admit to loving Swedish Fish. Each purchase wasn't large, but at that time, a total of $10 would have been a lot of money. We figured Mami would not notice and just pay the bill on the first of the month.

Of course, it did not go unnoticed. Papo showed her the ledger. Candy. Candy. Candy. That's what the ledger read. The inevitable occurred, and we found ourselves in BIG trouble when she figured out what her debt amounted to. We were grounded. End of Swedish Fish.

Mami eventually forgave us, but as a consequence, we were banned from buying unauthorized food, candy, or whatever, without her consent. Nonetheless, Mami would surprise us with candy—occasionally.

* * *

As a young lady, Mami had had that dream of becoming a registered nurse. Unfortunately, she wasn't given the opportunity to follow it. This was her frustration and perhaps the source of some of her anger. Her dream had been to finish high school, go to college, and study nursing. During her time in Puerto Rico, she worked for a hospital as a nursing assistant, even administering injections and working as a phlebotomist. She loved her job, and saw it as a path to her dream.

Be that as it may, my aunt (about 15 years older) sent for Mami to come to Milwaukee. Being a loyal sister, Mami packed her bags and, with little to no English skills, obeyed to her sister's request. As was the custom in most Latino families when help was needed, Mami felt obligated to take care of her sister's six children while her sister worked. Mami's dream faded away the instant she moved to a country where English was the dominant language, a language she never mastered. However, as fate would have it, even at the expense of her dreams, that move turned out to be beneficial to my sisters and me.

Shortly after Papi's arrival from Puerto Rico, he met and eventually married his first wife, Margaret. They had three boys. Mami was their babysitter. Papi and Margaret were married for several years before marital problems led to their divorce. It wasn't long after that he and Mami started dating and eventually married. Lo and behold, a move, a divorce, a love story, and three children later, our family was formed.

My parents were in love and inseparable. This was displayed in their candid public affection. Still, they did have a tumultuous marriage. It was a love/hate relationship. When they got along, we were a happy family. But when they fought, life at home was a struggle. Sadly, Mami's methods of dealing with Papi during fierce arguments extended to her children as well.

No doubt Mami loved us but she did have a little mean streak in her. She lived by the adage of "spare the rod, spoil the child." She might have taken that a little bit to the extreme. Perhaps that was how she had been raised. Therefore, it was how she would raise us. Tough love.

Like typical siblings, my sisters and I had our share of fights and arguments, which occasionally ended in something accidentally breaking. Instead of using the opportunity to talk to us and calm the emotions, we would get hit by thrown objects: a glass or anything that was in Mami's hand. When things were out of control in the home, she took her anger or frustration out on us. It was her way of discipline.

Mami, God rest her soul, had a rage in her. At times, she chose to discipline us with a belt or an extension cord or the occasional broom cracked over the head, and of course, I can't forget the infamous *chancletaso*, getting hit with a slipper! The *chancletaso* was the most common object used for discipline, and I would bet this was (and probably still is) the case in most Latino families. Physical discipline would be a normal occurrence in our family throughout the years.

On rare occasions (as highlighted by my sisters' experience) our mother would take her methods of discipline a bit too far. Once she swung a machete at me for riding my bike outside the boundaries of our neighborhood.

My sister, Dalila, and I, along with some friends, had decided to ride our bikes to the Lake Michigan lakefront, which was about five miles from home. As fate would have it, a family friend spotted us, and word got back to Mami rather quickly. When we arrived home, Mami was waiting for us on the porch and asked, "*¿A donde estaban?* Where were you?"

Out of fear, we lied and said we were at a friend's house. Mami, knowing this was a lie, waited until we were indoors, where she proceeded to discipline us the only way she knew how to. She grabbed the first object within her reach and given that she was chopping up sugarcane at the time, it was the machete. She grabbed it and said, "*Ven aqui.* Come here." She swung it towards me as I ran away from her. I don't believe her intent was to wound me. Instead, it was to strike fear in me and emphasize never again to disobey her rules regarding boundaries. Fear is what I felt at that moment.

Mami's rants were not limited to the home front. They extended outside the home as well. Dalila had come home from Holmes Elementary School with a black eye and temporal contusion. While leaving school, she was confronted by a girl who had bullied her throughout the year. Mami had always expressed, "*Si alguien te molesta, tu te defiendes, si no, vas a tener problemas conmigo.* If anyone messes with you, you'd better defend yourself or you will have problems with me."

Given the lose-lose position my sister was in, she decided to stand up for herself, rather than deal with Mami's wrath. Dalila stood her ground, ready to defend herself when out of nowhere, she was struck by another student and knocked to the ground while several girls proceeded to beat her. One of them kicked her in the head.

Administrators intervened and my sister was eventually sent home.

Mami was furious at the first sight of my sister's injuries. She immediately went to the school office, and in a fit of rage, slapped the first female student she saw. The girl she slapped had nothing to do with beating my sister. This was the vengeance Mami resorted to, therefore, she took it out on whomever was in her line of fire. It was an unfortunate circumstance for the student who was slapped. What this unfortunate student experienced is only a glimpse of the physical abuse my sisters and I endured. Regrettably, physical abuse was only one aspect of Mami's tactics. There was emotional and psychological castigation as well.

Mami bought a box of Band-Aids. I was maybe four or five years of age. She told my sister and me, "*Esto es para tapar rotitos*. This is for when you have a little hole, you cover it." She was referring to the body, of course, breaking the skin.

Mami left us alone in the house at times, which was safe because she knew the neighbors and relatives would keep an eye on us. During one such occasion, we remembered what she said about covering holes. We took it literally and, being that we had holes in our walls, we covered as many of them as the box of Band-Aids allowed us to do.

In our minds, we thought we were doing something helpful. We stood back proudly admiring our work and couldn't wait for Mami to see the repairs we had done to improve our home.

Talk about being on the wrong side of that notion. Mami came home and saw the Band-Aids all over the walls and immediately went into a meltdown. She asked, "Why are there Band-Aids on the walls?" We explained that we covered up all the *rotitos*. She didn't hit us. Instead, she took out a knife and said, "You don't know what a *rotito* is? Well, now I am going to show you what a *rotito* is."

She chased us around the house with a knife repeating that she was going to show us what a *rotito* was. We didn't have the mental capacity to know if she was trying to scare us or send us a message. It terrified us both as we ran away from her. It was yet another traumatic experience.

All along, we had thought we were doing something nice and helpful.

* * *

Nocturnal enuresis (bedwetting) is very common among children, and my sister Dalila and I were not spared this condition. It wouldn't be uncommon for either one of us to wet the bed on occasion. However, when my sister wet her bed, she would get up in the middle of the night and come to my bed. Lamentably, she would often wet my bed too, which made it seem like we had both wet our beds.

There are moments in life that remain ingrained in your mind and profoundly affect you both emotionally and mentally. Although there are plenty of others, the next two still resonate strongly.

Frustrated and unable to control our invariable bed-wetting, Mami would punish my sister and me by making us kneel in the basement on ridged bricks for several minutes.

As bedwetting continued, Mami would threaten that she was going to burn our buttocks if we didn't stop. Frustrated after yet another night of bedwetting, she turned on an electric burner, waited until it got red-hot, grabbed me, and pulled down my pants, threatening she was going to sit me on the red-hot burner. As she hovered me over the burner, I could feel the intense heat while screaming in terror believing I was going to be burned. Thankfully, she never went through with the threat. It was her way of trying to scare me. In fact, this fear probably made the bedwetting worse.

As one can imagine, stressed and afraid of what was clearly a condition we could not control, the tipping point came the day we were publicly humiliated as my sister and I were walking home from elementary school together with our friends. Our house was slightly set back, which blocked our view of what was awaiting us. As we neared home, from a distance everyone noticed what could only be described as purposeful degradation. Our mother had hung out my sister's white sheet besmirched with a large pee stain, displayed for everyone to see.

In a moment of shame and embarrassment, my sister ran to the house, and pulled down the sheet. The real stain was made to our emotional status, as all friends who witnessed this were now aware of our bed-wetting.

Sadly, moments like this not only occurred during times of mischievous behavior or circumstances out of our control, but in instances when something that merited praise or laughter induced the opposite.

* * *

While in first grade at Holmes Elementary School, my teacher announced, "A generous individual donated some clothes to us. Does anybody want to take clothes home?" In excitement, I raised my hand and stated, "I do." The donation was a couple pairs of pants and a shirt. The teacher wrapped them in brown construction paper, like a gift.

"Here you go Pascual," the teacher stated. It was the middle of winter. Excitedly, I ran home with my free clothes in hand, thinking Mami was going to be equally elated.

As I entered the house, I yelled in a proud voice, "*Mami, Mami, Mami, me dieron ropa, gratis*. I was given free clothes."

As I stood there, smiling from ear to ear, waiting for the affirmation that this was exciting news, the unexpected happened. She became enraged. She immediately spanked me and stripped off my clothes, threw me outside, and made me stand on the porch in my underwear. I stood there shivering in the frigid temperature, unable to understand how accepting free clothes would make her so angry. I stood on the porch for what seemed like an eternity, all the while not knowing what I had done wrong.

In dismay, I began crying and shaking. At that moment, I had never felt so alone. Shortly thereafter, Papi came home and saw me standing outside. Confused, he took me inside and I immediately ran to my room seeking comfort and warmth. I found that comfort with a blanket, not with my mother.

Papi questioned Mami about why I was outside without clothes. I overheard them arguing about the situation. Mami's justification was that people at school would think we were poor and in need of help (well, we were). She felt she needed to teach me a lesson. She was embarrassed. It was a pride thing.

It's important to emphasize that I don't want to characterize her as an uncompassionate mother who abused us daily. Unfortunately, when she became irate, she did direct her anger and frustration toward her children. Mami loved us and cared for us. Although her methods were a bit unorthodox, her heart was always strong in love for her family.

As I have advanced in my education and intellectual understanding of human behavior, I've come to the understanding that her actions were born out of her own painful past and her childhood upbringing. Hurt people, hurt people. My sisters and I endured the wrath of Mami's acrimonious moments of distress. Despite this, Mami loved us tremendously and we reciprocated that love for her.

* * *

Papi loved his family as well. I remember being spanked by him once, which was, in reality, only a light tap on the rear end. Other than that, he never laid a hand on me. He was definitely not the disciplinarian.

However, he was not without his flaws.

We often went to Chicago to visit family. On one of those visits, Papi decided to head to the bar he frequently patronized while in that city. In typical fashion, he took me along, given my love for shooting pool. Mami decided to stay back with our relatives.

After several games of pool, I walked over to where Papi had been sitting. To my surprise, he wasn't there. I looked around and carefully scanned the room in hopes of spotting him. He was nowhere to be found. The bartender noticed my concerned look and said, "He went out that way," as he pointed to the exit door.

I stepped outside, only to find our car gone. Papi had left me behind, alone in an unfamiliar city. He had forgotten all about me.

This wouldn't be the last time he left me.

As I sat on the edge of the sidewalk, not knowing what to do, my only recourse was to cry out for Mami.

The story goes that upon returning to the house, Mami asked, "*¿Dónde está Pocholito?* Where is Pocholito?" Papi's immediate, stunned facial expression said it all. She instantly knew he had forgotten me.

Moments later, a car approached, screeching around the corner toward me. It was my parents! Mami jumped out of the car, crying as she hugged and kissed me, elated I was okay. As for Papi, the distance between Chicago and Milwaukee is approximately 90 miles, but that day, it seemed like 190 miles given he had to listen to Mami's exasperated rant at what had occurred for the entire drive home.

* * *

Papi was a hard worker. However, he also liked to have fun. Of course, I liked to join in on that fun. When given the chance, I spent my days fishing, playing baseball, shooting pool, and playing an instrument while listening to my favorite music, Salsa. My love of these pastimes is a direct result of my time spent with Papi, who either taught me or spent time in the art of these activities.

Much of Papi's and my time during the summer was spent fishing. This was a weekly occurrence with us, a great bonding experience. We owned a small motor boat, which we often used for our fishing escapades. Papi taught me how to hook a worm and set a bobber, how to be patient while the line is cast, and that it is okay for hours to pass without a catch because there's always next time. It didn't matter if we were lucky enough to hook a fish, although the impact of a successful catch was admittedly pure elation. Fishing provided a form of closeness for Papi and me, a chance to spend quality time together. I learned that patience truly is a virtue and to truly enjoy the outdoors.

Fishing from the boat gave me that sense of thrilling excitement. However, the excitement took on a whole new meaning one summer day at Phantom Lake. We were enjoying an afternoon picnic with family and friends. After several rounds of riding in the boat with Papi, I asked, "*Papi dejame sacar el bote.* Let me take the boat out. *Yo se manejar lo.* I know how to drive it." Shockingly, he tossed me the keys. Here was an eight-year-old boy being handed the keys to a motorized boat, so I instantly darted toward the boat before he could change his mind. Clearly Mami was not paying attention at that moment. I jumped into the boat, turned it on, and off I went.

I had no clue what I was doing, but was eager to start my self-tour of Phantom Lake. So, there I went with the throttle fully engaged. Mami finally noticed what had occurred. On the pier, she was yelling at Papi and frantically flailing her arms, desperately trying to get my attention.

All the while, I was having a blast. Little did I realize I could have injured myself and anyone else in the water. I was oblivious to my surroundings. I ultimately saw Mami jumping up and down trying to get my attention and I knew I was in trouble. My tour of Phantom Lake came to an end, sad for me, but probably good for those in the water. Hesitantly, I headed back. As I docked the boat, surprisingly, she didn't yell at me but grabbed and hugged me as she stared into Papi's eyes with contempt.

Papi was never in panic mode. He said, "*Él tiene que aprender*. He has got to learn." The only lesson reinforced that day was for Papi. You put Mami's babies in harm's way and you will pay the price.

* * *

Papi loved our family (he had three other sons but I don't recall that he had a close relationship with them). I fondly remember our moments of spending quality time together. As a matter of fact, I would define us as having a strong family nucleus. It was not uncommon for Mami and Papi to play hide-and-go-seek with us, as well as other games and activities. One in particular was a traditional Puerto Rican song and dance named *Ambos a Dos*. We stood in two lines facing each other, singing the lyrics while walking towards each other.

In addition, we were fortunate enough to be able to visit the Wisconsin Dells and Dandelion Park at least once a year. Dandelion Park was a small-scale amusement park, compared to the likes of Great America. It was a treat we relished; Mami and Papi allowed us to ride the rides all day until exhaustion. Wisconsin Dells trips usually consisted of a day or two of camping and visiting the local attractions.

As with the boat experience, Papi allowed me to do things on my own as a way of building independence and self-reliance, concepts Mami struggled with at times. This independence instilled confidence in me that today is still prevalent in my life. I don't fear the unknown but welcome the challenge it brings. Like gambling, but not in its traditional sense.

Dad played *bolita**, the underground Pick Three Lottery. *Bolita* (little ball) was a humble man's numbers game which came out of Chicago. Every Wednesday, the *bolita* guy (bookie) would make his rounds in the neighborhood, collecting numbers and money from his customers. If you won, he took 10% of your winnings.

As was customary, Papi would wait on the porch for the *bolita* guy so he could make his picks for the week. One day, Papi decided to let me in on the fun. He asked me, "*¿Quiere jugar?* Want to play?" I said, "*Si.*" He said, "*Dale un numero para jugar.* Give me a number to play."

"*Quiero jugar el número 344.* I want the number 344."

I don't know where that number came from, I just blurted it out. As luck would have it, that number hit. I heard Papi yell out in a loud voice, "*Los pegamos.* We hit the number!" He used the words *los pegamos*, when in reality I was the one who had provided the winning number. He really should have stated, "*Pocholito, te pegaste!* You hit the number." Wishful thinking on my end, I guess. I think the jackpot was close to $2,000. Not bad for a small-time numbers game.

With the winnings, my parents bought me a dirt bike. Of course, I thought it was the coolest present I had ever received. It was lime green and in my eyes looked like a real motorcycle with a plastic tank in front. For a boy from an impoverished community to receive a new bike, well, I was the envy of the block, to say the least. And for a brief moment, I was the happiest kid in the neighborhood. I rode that bike tirelessly for the two weeks I had it.

---

*Bolita was one of the mob's most profitable rackets in history until states made it legal and called it a lottery. Bolita had 100 numbered balls which were placed in a bag that was thrown from person to person until time for drawing when the person holding the bag drew out the winning number. People made bets at the local grocery store, the butcher, in the street, at work, and in any number of bars, cafes, and restaurants. Millions of people bet their money on what the combination of the balls would be. The thing was, most of the games were fixed. Tricks such as using 100 balls with the same number. Scams such as putting winning numbers on ice before the game to make them easier for the selector to find when reaching into the bag. Also the selector would hide the winning balls in his hand then 'find them' in the bag. During the mid-60's many clubs in Chicago...were used for gambling games and operations. The Tropicana Nightclub and the Bamboo club had Bolita games every night and were attended mostly by Puerto Ricans. http://www.gangsterbb.net/threads/ubbthreads.php?ubb=showflat&Number=747877

Unbelievably, I left it on the porch one night and as fate would have it, the next morning, it was gone. I was dumbfounded and heartbroken. My one prized possession was gone. I cried inconsolably for hours.

In an act of sympathy, Papi did one of the most amazing things that helped heal my broken heart. He surprised me with a Yamaha 250 mini-motorcycle. Let me say that again...he bought me a motorcycle! A silver gas-powered motorcycle with a black seat.

If the boys on the block had been envious of my dirt bike, the motorcycle took it over the top. What a streak of good fortune!

Papi taught me all the nuances of riding my motorcycle. I was a quick learner and ready to ride into the wind. During this time, we lived on the second floor above the *bodega*, so needless to say it was an adventure pushing it up and down the stairs. Papi, without complaint, would take on that task. Fortunately, the funeral home next door had a large parking lot where I would ride without fear of crashing or injuring myself on the busy street. Papi allowed me to ride in that parking lot as long as I wanted, or until the owner of the funeral home asked me to leave. Either way, I was not allowed to leave the perimeter of the parking lot, as I was underage.

I was sort of a little daredevil and desired speed. To feed that desire, Mami and Papi would pack a lunch, and we would head over to the nearby Humane Society, which was at the time was located off of Estabrook Park on Milwaukee's north side. There was a large dirt road behind the building that provided the opportunity to ride with a little bit of reckless abandonment, but safe enough to reduce the possibility of injury. My parents would make themselves comfortable on a blanket and enjoy their lunch. Meanwhile, I was having the time of my life, imagining myself as a young Puerto Rican Evel Knievel.

I reveled in the feeling of freedom and excitement that the motorcycle gave me. While my room was always messy, I made sure to keep my most prized possession sparkling clean, religiously polishing it daily with the utmost care. It was kept in my room, in my sight, never to be left on the porch. Lesson learned.

There are pockets of time where the most unforgettable memories are created. In all my boyish experiences, owning that motorcycle, as brief a time that it was, created unequivocal memories that offset the emotional unbalanced trials and tribulations of my adverse childhood experiences.

Reflections

- How has your childhood shaped your adulthood experience?

- How can you use that experience to shape the lives of others?

INNING 4

CURVEBALL

It was a warm spring day in May of 1977. I asked to be sent home from school because I had a stomach ache.

In all honesty, I wanted to go home and do what most kids desire most—play. At my request and persistence, the school nurse called Mami to inform her of my perceived condition, to which Mami gave her permission to send me home. I was ecstatic as I went on my way, joyful as could be, all the while not knowing what was awaiting me at home.

It would be the last time I was genuinely and playfully happy and emotionally secure for years to come.

There are moments in life that change everything from what is seemingly normal to what is clearly abnormal, especially when seen through the eyes of a ten-year-old boy trying to make sense of the incomprehensible.

The generational hand-me-down belief in *brujeria* (witchcraft) is the cornerstone for my perspective on the following events.

I believe this event was the cause of my subsequent experiences of abuse, abandonment, neglect, and iniquity. This moment was the first sign of a tumultuous downward fall for our family. I don't have any scientific proof that this was the cause of what followed, but in my heart, I believe it to be the inauguration to our family unit's demise and dysfunctionality.

As I said, it was a normal spring day in May. Uncharacteristically, I had not wanted to go to school. Go figure. I was a good student—I did my work, excelled in math, and was very adept at playing sports. For the most part, I loved going to school. It was a place I felt safe.

Mami had initially denied my request to stay home from school that morning, so off I went, albeit begrudgingly. I told my teacher, "I have a stomach ache." The school nurse checked my temperature and found nothing wrong other than my stomach ache complaint.

I asked her, "Can you please call my mom?" She acquiesced and did. Surprisingly, Mami said, "Send him home."

It was a four- or five-block walk home. I played up the sick role until I got around the corner, and out of sight of the school, when I was in the clear. I thought about what I was going to do with the rest of my day. Maybe I'd shine my motorcycle. Could I get the motorcycle downstairs myself? Probably not because Papi was working, besides that, I was supposed to be sick. I was planning out my day, but most importantly, I wondered how I was going to convince Mami to let me go out and play when my friends got home from school. My skipping turned into a fast pace as I was nearing home. All the while, I acknowledged that it was a beautiful day to play strike-out! My master plan was in full effect, but admittedly in its infancy stage.

Once home, Mami told me to go to my room and lie down. I went in and closed the door. That was fine with me. I was playing with my toys while trying to be quiet so Mami wouldn't hear me.

Our apartment above the bodega consisted of a living room, dining room, and hallway that connected the bedrooms and bathroom. Within the kitchen was a smaller room that was used as my bedroom.

The color scheme was beige. The walls were adorned with pictures of Puerto Rico and there were figurines of roosters throughout the living room. Mami had an affinity for roosters, perhaps because they reminded her of the island she had left behind. There was also the mandatory picture of *The Last Supper*; the one every Latino family had hanging in their home.

Plastic covered the couches, lampshades, and fabric on the dining room chairs. Fortunately, due to cost, we couldn't afford to have all the furniture covered, therefore leaving a few odd pieces of furniture unprotected. My fellow Latino brothers and sisters know this not to be anything out of the ordinary, given most families invested in protecting their furniture with this infamous covering. Although the plastic did provide that protective layer, there was a downside to it. During those hot summer days when the temperature rose above 80 degrees, you found your bare legs sticking to the plastic as you attempted to peel yourself off. In retrospect, Mami should have covered our mattresses with plastic given our propensity to wet the bed. However, who wants to experience the sound and feel of plastic as one sleeps? Certainly not me.

While keeping myself occupied, Mami came to my room and said, "*Ven aqui.* Come out here." As I walked out of my bedroom, she told me someone was going to pray for my stomach ache. Afraid of the consequences for lying, I couldn't bring myself to confess to not having one, so I went along with this so-called prayer.

This nature of prayer wasn't anything out of the ordinary in the Latino community. Many still do this today. When Puerto Rican (and other Latino) Catholics buy a new house (or car), traditionally a priest or pastor will be invited over for dinner. He will then bless the house or other possessions, to protect the family from potential harm. In addition, a priest was also asked to pray over an ill loved one.

We were "holiday Catholics," which tells you we didn't attend church regularly. We had no parish priest to invite over, however that didn't stop Mami from following this tradition. She had found someone willing to come to the apartment to pray for our home, as well as my fictitious stomach ache.

Walking into the living room, there stood the woman (I believe) who would change the course of our family history.

Her hair was wildly matted, held in place by a bandana. She wore a long, bright, colorful dress. Her neck was adorned with beads—religious necklaces like a cross or rosary—and dangling earrings. She appeared haggard and unkempt. Her presence felt out of the ordinary. Next to her belongings were some containers, one of which held some sort of oil. I stood there feeling uncomfortable by her strange and enchanted appearance.

Mami said, "*Quédate ahí.* Stand there. *Ella va a orar por tu estómago.* She is going to pray for your stomach."

The strange woman began reciting (what seemed to me) an unusual prayer, during which she rubbed my stomach with the oil and started speaking in tongues. The eccentricity of it all was deeply weird and then her unexpected sneeze added to the odd disposition.

What made the sneeze odd? Mucus (snot) gushed from her nostrils and dangled in mid air. I didn't have a real stomach ache until that point, but now I felt sick. In fact, I was grossed out. I thought, *Something doesn't feel right.*

I looked at Mami and she stared back at me. This strange woman, unbothered, continued praying as the thick mucus dangled down her face and below her chin. My mouth agape, I continued looking at Mami and thought, *Is she going to wipe herself?* Shockingly, she didn't.

The woman stood there in a trance-like state. I couldn't for the life of me understand why she wouldn't take a tissue and clean herself, and then move on. Nonetheless, the praying continued for what seemed like an eternity. During this strange besiegement, it was unclear for what and to whom she was praying.

I once again looked at Mami in the hope of some sort of bailout but her facial expression instructed me not to move. I reluctantly stood in place, waiting for this grotesque situation to end.

The prayer finally concluded. She cleaned herself up and carried on as if nothing unusual had just occurred. Finally Mami said, "*Vuelve a tu habitación.* Go back to your room."

As quickly as I was able to, I headed back to my room with a strange feeling coupled with a bit of fear and confusion. I knew what I had just experienced was unnatural, unpleasant, and it made me very uncomfortable.

Throughout my childhood, there have been instances where I believe God intervened in my life. Given this faith, I knew the voice inside of me was guided by the faith that God was protecting me from wrongdoing. It was intuition that led me to believe this so-called prayer had been, in some way, counter to God's blessings.

Although I wasn't a church-goer, I did occasionally go to church with my Pentecostal cousins. There, I saw people filled with the Holy Spirit and speaking in tongues, minus the (mucus) snot converging from their nostrils. In fact, during their moments of being filled with the Holy Spirit, I never felt uncomfortable. Conversely, I felt peace, joy, and a sense of spirituality.

Back in my room, I was still shaken by the experience. The woman proceeded to speak in tongues as she walked through our house, roaming from room to room. Thankfully, she did not step into my room. Shortly thereafter, the front door closed and immediately, silence permeated the apartment.

I waited a while after her departure before stepping out of my room. I cautiously looked around as my gut told me something was not right. This gut feeling strengthened and confirmed my misgiving when I saw blood smeared over every door frame.

I immediately asked Mami, "Why is there blood on our doorways?" She nonchalantly responded, *"Eso es sangre de Cabra.* It is goat's blood." No other explanation.

When Dalila came home from school, she too was shocked to see the blood. "What's going on?" Intuitively, I thought, *Is the blood there to bring in good spirits? Was the woman blessing the house?* Mami discounted the blood, explaining that it was simply a prayer. "Someone came and prayed for our home."

Was this woman there to bless our home or was she there practicing *brujeria*? *Brujeria* is tantamount to voodoo. Demonology, folk magic, and some occult practices are part of this dark Latin American tradition. In *brujeria*, goats are sacrificed, and their blood used to bring spirits to do their bidding. Was the woman a *bruja*? Was this supposed to be an exorcism of some kind to pray away evil spirits? Did she present herself as bringing good but ultimately brought evil to our family?

Before that fateful day, my family, despite all of our dysfunctionality, was a family unit. We loved one another. We were there for one another.

Be that as it may, for one reason or another, Mami suspected Papi was having an affair. She had no proof of this; however, she did have a suspicion. My sisters and I were oblivious to any potential marital strife. In retrospect, was this suspicion the reason she requested this woman to pray over our home?

I have a strong belief that things happen for a reason. For that matter, it wasn't a coincidence that I was there for the event that took place. I have always wondered why I hadn't wanted to go to school that particular day. *Why did I pretend I had a stomach ache? Why did my coming home overlap with this strange woman and her ritual, or whatever it was?*

Perhaps I would have come home, seen the blood, wondered why it was there, then gone about my business, like my sister Dalila had. Was I there to better understand the downward transformation of my family in the coming years?

It would be many years later that I would make the connection. Not long after this juncture, I witnessed a 180-degree change in our family dynamics. Sadly, my parents separated later that same year, and as a means of comfort, Mami turned to alcohol, which quickly escalated to alcoholism. The life I had known was turned completely upside down. Although it may have been sunny outdoors that day I came home early from school, a dark cloud prevailed over our home and in our lives.

Over the next several chapters, I hope to provide a sense of plausibility for subsequent family events.

Reflections

- How have outside influences impacted your childhood, whether positively or negatively?

- How have you used those experiences to help others?

INNING 5

DEEP "DRIVE" AND GONE

*T*attletale. Of all the great qualities my sister Dalila had, this one wasn't her most endearing. My sister knew all the family secrets (at least she thought she did) and was ever eager to share with anyone and everyone willing to listen. It wasn't done to be malicious, but just as one would expect from an inquisitive, energetic pre-teen.

The November day that Papi left, Dalila was in the living room when he picked up the rotary dial phone with the long trailing spiral cord. He walked into the bedroom, closing the door behind him. As he engaged in a whispered and somewhat surreptitious conversation, Dalila was listening although she could not hear the details of the phone call. That call and Dalila's inquisitive nature would eventually be the catalyst that spiraled our family into a future of uncertainty. In retrospect, the signs of uncertainty were present long before that decisive phone call.

Papi's behavior over the previous several months had seemed erratic. Arguments between my parents had become more and more common, even physical at times: pushing, pulling, and/or shoving each other. We kids witnessed an escalation of needless arguing and bickering, more so than ever. Our instinct told us something was going on, however, we were raised not to ask questions regarding adult issues.

For instance, after a night out at the local bar, my parents began arguing on their way home, which then led to a physical altercation. As they entered the house, Mami could be heard saying, "You don't know what pain is. Do you want to see what pain is?" In an instant, she reached for the switchblade (which she always kept in her purse) and began slicing her forearm. She unintentionally hit a vein.

Horrified, Dalila and I began crying and screaming and begging Mami to stop. Needless to say, we were shocked and terrified. It's hard to put into words the feeling of fear we both felt that night. Obviously, it was something no child should ever have to witness. We were no different.

Seeing the blood gushing from Mami's arm, Papi immediately grabbed the switchblade, stopping her from causing greater harm. "¿*Qué te hace mujer?* Woman, what are you doing?" He quickly wrapped her arm in a towel and off they went to the emergency room. Little did we understand that each strike of the blade across Mami's forearm served as a metaphor of a perplexed marriage on the verge of a distressing separation.

Their relationship was quickly falling apart and it was getting the best of Mami. Her emotional and heightened rage was greater than her self-control. When the rage happened, she would lose all sense of reality, reacting without any concern for her own well-being and that of her loved ones.

Dalila and I tried to manage through it all as best we could, hiding the pain. My daily escapes had been playing strike-out on the flat brick wall at the side of the *bodega* or riding my bike aimlessly as a means of avoidance. Anything to get away from the realities of what was happening at home. I was eager to start fifth grade that fall. Eager to spend time with friends, play sports, and plunge into a structured classroom setting.

* * *

Allow me to take you back to that "decisive" phone call. As Papi stepped out of the room, he saw Dalila standing nearby. I'm certain he knew that it was only a matter of time before she shared this information with someone, in particular with Mami. He said, "*¿No le digas nada a tu madre sobre la llamada!* Don't mention anything to your mother regarding the phone call." Followed by, "*Por que estaba escuchando?* Why were you listening? *Que oirste?* What did you hear?"

Dalila played it off by saying she hadn't heard anything, which was true because he had been whispering. However, in typical Dalila fashion, the minute Mami came home, she spilled the beans. "*Mami, Mami, Papi estaba en el telephono.* Papi was on the phone, inside the bedroom, and he was whispering."

In Dalila's mind, she was sharing information she thought Mami should know. She was a 12-year-old *entrometida*—an overly curious, nosy young lady. Later, she would feel guilty, afraid that her antics had been the cause of Papi's departure. She wasn't responsible, of course. The Bible teaches us that what happens in the dark will eventually come to light. No truer words were ever spoken.

Mami and Papi made their way to the bedroom. From there, the situation intensified and an argument ensued as Mami began asking questions, starting to put the puzzle pieces together. Perhaps feeling cornered and unable to think of an excuse, Papi confessed to having an affair and announced he was leaving.

As one can imagine, Mami was devastated. She was angry, crying, and screaming as fear set in. Carrying his suitcase, Papi walked across the living room where Dalila and I sat tearfully watching him from the couch, waiting for him to say something, anything. Without so much as a glance our way, he walked toward the door. Perhaps it was the guilt of what he was leaving behind that stopped him from uttering a single word. We too were fearful. Why was our father leaving? What was happening to our family?

Mami, in a desperate attempt to save her marriage, hung on to Papi's leg, "*No te valles, no te valles.* Don't leave, Don't leave." Regardless of the affair, Mami was willing to forgive him and work to salvage their marriage.

Papi's mind was made up. He wanted out; he had had enough. Annoyed, he kicked Mami in the face, head, and shoulders attempting to loosen her from his leg. After multiple blows, she finally let go, and Papi walked out the door.

Instinctively, I leapt off the couch and followed him, not realizing I was barefoot.

Although it was snowing, my bare feet were not affected. I was on a mission to stop Papi from leaving. Racing down the 15 to 20 steps from the second floor felt like an eternity. I was torn and desperate. Whom should I choose? In that instance, I decided to follow Papi, knowing Dalila would help Mami.

In a desperate attempt to change his mind, I pleaded, "*Papi, no te valles.* Dad, please don't go. Please don't leave." To no avail. He did not once look back or acknowledge my pleas. I felt invisible, rejected by the one person I saw as my hero.

Keys in hand, Papi walked to his Cadillac, opened the trunk, and threw his luggage in, all the while ignoring my cries. Without hesitation, he got in and started the engine. He did not simply drive off; he accelerated at a high pace, causing his snow-covered car to shower me with a downpour of snow. I stood there, stunned and snow-drenched, as I watched him drive away. As much as I wanted to, I couldn't get my legs to move. The taillights faded in the snowy haze as I stood in the middle of the road. In an instant, he was gone.

Although there was no correlation, my mind flashed back to the time I had inadvertently been left behind at the Chicago bar, except then, he returned after realizing his mistake. No mistake this time. I was left standing in the street alone. He was accelerating away from me. No explanation, no "*Lo siento mijó,* I am sorry, my son." I was left with the snowy silence and fading taillights.

Papi was gone. Gone was my fishing partner, my baseball buddy, and my hero.

Reluctantly, I made my way back to the house, occasionally looking over my shoulder to see if perhaps he would return. My barefoot walk was slow as I headed toward the door. I was shivering from the combination of cold, snow, and fear. I began thinking, *What am I going to find when I get upstairs?*

Not surprisingly, as I neared the top of the stairs, the sounds of crying and yelling could be heard. Mami needed somewhere to direct her anger, hurt, and confusion. She found that in Dalila. I walked in as Mami was shaking her and stating, "This is your fault."

Oddly, neither my sister nor I can recall the rest of that night. For all we know, the emotional intensity perhaps kicked in, I suppose, protecting us from further distress and emotional damage. I only remember hardly sleeping as images kept replaying in my head. A flurry of questions raced through my mind. *What is going on? Why did that happen? Does Papi no longer love us? What did Mami do? What did we do? What did I do? Had I somehow caused this?*

I woke up the next morning, hoping it was just a bad dream, only to realize that Papi was, in fact, gone. Life as I had known it changed overnight and would never return to what had been normal. Mami was distraught. Her eyelids were swollen. There were visible dark circles under her eyes, from what I assume was lack of sleep, in addition to the multiple blows to her body the night before.

In a way, we lost both our parents that night. We still had Mami's physical presence, however, she would soon become emotionally detached for the next eight to ten years.

• * *

Mami attempted to find answers. She made some calls, as well as asked around. She had to know who this other woman was. This quest did not come at an easy price. It took most of her attention and consequently her parental responsibilities as well. This behavior did not go unnoticed within our family circle. One of our older cousins decided to step in and take matters into his own hands. He removed us from our home to spare us further neglect. He knew we were not being fed, although not to the point of starvation. More so, we lacked and missed Mami's home-cooked meals.

We lasted about 24 hours with our cousin before we both wanted to go home. "Are you sure?" "Yes." Despite Mami's actions, we worried about her. We knew in our hearts that our place was by her side. Papi had left her, and we were damned if we were going to do that as well, even if that meant our commitment was not reciprocated. Mami didn't realize it at that time, but she needed us as much as we needed her.

Although children have a natural ability to be resilient, they should not be required to fend for themselves. How did we survive in our impoverished and neglected environment? Community. Period.

My aunt's home was always open and there I was able to eat the home-cooked Puerto Rican meals I so desired and longed for. Her grandson, my cousin, Juan Carlos, was my best friend. Spending time with him was a means of escape, as well as an opportunity to make fond memories. Their home was my safe haven.

Parents of my neighborhood friends were also privy to our situation at home. I strategically showed up for visits to their homes around dinnertime. To my luck, but mostly due to their sympathy, I was never denied a meal. These small acts of kindness helped to sustain me, and they have never been forgotten.

Unfortunately, not everyone looked at us with sympathy and understanding. Some friends were no longer allowed to hang around with us for fear that we would have a negative impact on them. Left alone physically and emotionally, Dalila and I had a lot of freedom. We stayed out all hours of the day and night. We lacked structure and comfort when we needed it most. Mami turned to alcohol as a means of comfort, and indirectly turned away from the support of her family.

* * *

Over the years, Dalila and I endured Mami's anger and depression. Failed suicide attempts only heightened our insecurities and increased our fear of abandonment. Perhaps the emotional pain was too much for Mami to bear, or maybe it was an attempt to gain attention. Regardless of the reason, she was seeking a means of escape, while Dalila and I were seeking comfort and safety.

We were at a crisis point, but also had an innate sense of survival. There was something within me even as a child—wisdom perhaps—that said, *This isn't the way it is supposed to be. This is wrong.*

* * *

I had just come home from school, and as usual, sat on the couch with a bowl of cereal to watch cartoons. I noticed something odd. Mami was seated across the room on the love seat with a knife in her hand. She had an almost evil look on her face. I quickly called out to her, "Mami?"

No response. Once again, I called her, to no avail. Shortly thereafter, she began repeatedly striking the couch with the knife in a stabbing motion. She began mumbling incognizable words. Her aggression intensified with every strike.

Fearfully, I arose from the couch and went outside. Afraid to say anything, I attempted to erase what I just experienced through play and laughter.

A few hours later, I returned home, unsure of what I was going to find. Mami was lying on the large couch. My initial reaction was relief; I thought things were back to normal.

When I looked more closely, though, I saw she was foaming at the corner of her mouth and grunting. I stood frozen and unable to move, while shock and disbelief settled in. When my senses revived, I screamed out to my sisters, who had both just returned home. They immediately attempted to wake Mami as I ran across the street to alert my uncles and three older cousins who returned with me. They called out her name but Mami became more agitated and the foaming and grunting increased. Given my family's religious practices, they began to pray over her. The more they prayed, the more distressed Mami became. Her aggressiveness was so intense that with one sweep of her arm, she picked up my 200-pound cousin and tossed him against the wall.

Dalila jumped over the recliner like a gazelle leaping in fear of a predator. She landed on the floor, crouched with her knees clutched against her chest, and began screaming.

Events like this are difficult to erase and that day holds an indelible memory—another piece of the fabric of our childhood story.

Eventually, Mami quieted down. When she fully awakened and became aware of her surroundings, she looked perplexed and asked, "*¿Qué hacen aquí?* What are you guys doing here?" They replied, "*Estabas poseída.* You were possessed." As hard as she tried, Mami could not comprehend what they were talking about and likewise, neither could we.

There was little we could do to avert her continuing deterioration.

Deep "Drive" and Gone

* * *

I learned to depend on God at an early age and I inherently believed that he would intervene and answer my prayers. This belief would be the pillar I leaned on in two crucial moments in my life, first when I was about eight years old.

Innately, I was a good athlete with an ability to run fast. While in elementary school, I developed a respiratory condition that prevented me from running more than 10 or 15 feet without becoming extremely short of breath. Because I was not taken to see a doctor, it remained undiagnosed and worsened. Once I began coughing, it was difficult to catch my breath. Usually, each episode lasted five to ten minutes. Whether playing at school or home, the coughing and shortness of breath were triggered by physical activity. Ultimately feeling so frustrated and helpless, I locked my bedroom door, knelt down, and tearfully begged God to please take this breathing problem away.

I don't recall having another breathing episode thereafter.

The second critical incident happened when Mami, estranged from Papi, started seeking the company of others who might not have had our family's best interests in mind. One in particular was a woman I later found out was a prostitute. Mami, seeking friendship, allowed the woman to move in. She welcomed the woman into our home. I soon noticed suspicious behavior. Strange men began visiting our home both during the day and night. I wasn't sure what was going on, but something inside of me knew it was wrong. It felt eerie. I was afraid for my safety and my family's well being. I felt compelled to seek God's merciful guidance once again. I knelt in prayer and asked God to remove this woman from our home. I firmly believe my prayer was answered. With no explanation, the following day, the woman told my mother, "I think I am going to leave and live with

57

someone else." She packed her bags and left. The power of prayer sustains me to this day.

* * *

After Papi left, there were other consequences stemming from his absence. My Yamaha 250 motorcycle was the one prized possession I had reminding me of my memories with my father. It had been our father-son connection. I continued to love Papi through that bike even as it became nothing more than a fixture in my room. I still polished it daily.

Coming home from a nearby park one day, I turned the corner of Brown and Holton streets, only to find two men loading my motorcycle into a van.

I yelled, "What are you doing?"

One of the men said, "*Habla con tu madre*. Talk to your mother." There I stood, helpless, as the one last object connecting me with Papi was taken away.

I was crushed, not so much about the physical loss of the motorcycle, but by the emotional loss.

Mami had sold it. She sold my bike to buy alcohol.

* * *

Shortly thereafter, we moved across the street from where we had been living above the *bodega*. In the beginning, I was happy to leave the place that continuously reminded me of sad and disappointing moments. In my mind, this was an opportunity to push the reset button. Lamentably, that perpetual dark cloud continued to linger over our lives.

We moved to the second floor of the duplex, although which floor we lived on isn't that important. It was what I had to endure there on four different occasions that matters.

As the pain of Papi's abrupt departure continued to weigh heavily on Mami's psyche, signs of depression became evident.

Neither our family nor our circle of friends had the knowledge, or wherewithal, to seek treatment for depression.

John Maxwell states, "Crisis is a matter of perspective; how we view things determines how we do things" (Maxwell, 2013). Mami could see no end in sight. Her view was distorted by her emotional disconnect from reality, so she tried to resolve her depression by attempting to take her own life.

Mami's tipping point boiled over on a summer afternoon. I had invited some friends over to the house. As I opened the front door, located at the bottom of the staircase, there was an immediate and intense smell of gas. Not quite clear about what was going on, I asked my friends to leave. As I climbed the stairs, the smell of gas got increasingly stronger. There was no response as I called out for Mami.

I walked into the kitchen and once again stood there not comprehending what I was seeing. Mami had taken all the racks out of the old stove-top oven, turned on the gas pilots with no flame, closed all the windows, and physically laid as much of her body as possible inside the oven. Shocked, confused, and fearful, I took action as best as an eleven-year-old boy could do.

I pulled her out and struggled to carry her to the living room couch. No surprise; she was heavily intoxicated. Then it hit me. She was trying to end her life.

This was the first of four separate occasions, when I would smell gas, run in, immediately turn off the gas, drag her out of the oven, carry her, and lay her on the couch. Instinctively, I opened all the windows and let the house air out. While most eleven-year-olds were out playing and catching up with friends, I was interrupting Mami's suicide attempts.

Fear and anxiety raced through my veins each time I moved her to the couch, intoxicated and unaware of what was going on. Looking back on those events, my guess is the good Lord was watching over her. I always seemed to get home at the right time, just when the smell of gas had permeated through the house, but before it affected her physically. God must have led me home.

* * *

Before Papi left, I had been a good student. I especially liked math and was told I was an excellent speller. I don't recall being a troublemaker or for that matter being sent to the principal's office for disciplinary issues. Sure, I had my share of fist fights, but mostly to defend myself. Some classmates picked on me because I wore clothes bought from Goodwill. Back then, Goodwill stapled its price tags on the collar. Those staple marks were a dead giveaway. I could deal with the teasing and jokes, however, when physically charged, my recourse was to defend myself.

As fifth grade rolled on, the struggle to stay focused began to take its toll. I was present physically but mentally I was somewhere else. My grades plummeted. Intellectually, I was nowhere near meeting the curriculum expectations.

Homework took a back seat to the trials of home life. School was no longer a priority. Survival was. My thoughts focused on questions like, *What am I going to eat? Where am I going to eat?*

To make matters worse, no one at school seemed to notice. My grades were slipping, yet the why was not being addressed. I came to think that no one cared about me at school or at home so why should I care? From the age of ten on, Mami did not attend any parent conferences and never asked me about schoolwork; that simply wasn't on her radar.

I made it through fifth, sixth, and seventh grades with minimal effort. I believe it was the falseness of social advancement— move 'em along and eventually he will drop out. This set me up for failure. In essence, they were putting the educational future in the hands of a misguided and emotionally neglected child.

I was enrolled at Kosciuszko Middle School, but no sooner had I started than I became academically disengaged. I attended two months out of the ten-month school year. When I did attend, I did not do any classwork or homework. Unlike my earlier years, I now began acting out, being disruptive, and taking on the role of class clown attempting to disguise the pain and deflect from what I was not doing and what I didn't have. Years later, a psychotherapist revealed that I used humor to mask my sadness and emotions. This was a concept I had difficulty accepting for fear of facing my past.

School became a joke. I became a joke. I got kicked out of class a lot and was sent to the principal's office where I got yelled at and suspended on several occasions. The middle school administrators undoubtedly assumed I was an undisciplined child. Perhaps the trajectory of my life would have been diverted down a promising path if one teacher, counselor, or administrator had ever taken the time to ask me, "Why are you consistently missing class?" Or, "Is anything wrong?" Or, "Do you need anything?"

The truth was my real focus was on what was going to happen to Mami each day. *Was she going to be okay? Would she be passed out? Was I going to walk into a house full of gas? Was she going to be alive?* I typically found myself meandering around the school grounds not attending class except for lunch which, in many cases, was the only meal I would have for the day.

Life did not matter for Mami, so one can imagine her sense of responsibility for her children was not a high priority.

How did I avoid following the wrong path? Why didn't I join a gang to find the equivalent of family as some kids do? I did have friends who were in gangs. The Latin Kings and Spanish

Cobras were the local gangs. They did not interest me. Something within me knew that was not the path I wanted to follow. I did not allow myself to succumb to peer pressures. I consider myself lucky that something was guiding me. What it was, I was not sure. I've never tried drugs. They were certainly offered to me and used in my presence: marijuana to cocaine. I always turned them down. Drinks? Sure, occasionally when a friend's parents were gone, we would have a shot here and there. But that was a rare occurrence. For one thing, I couldn't afford to buy alcohol. Most importantly, Mami's indulgence hovered over my consciousness. I saw the damage alcohol was doing to her. Regrettably, as in the case with most kids who come from alcoholic families, wounds of alcoholism not only affect the alcoholic, they also have a reverberating impact on their children.

Case in point, a few neighborhood kids, unbeknownst to me, shared a common joke (nobody likes to be the butt of jokes). They would occasionally repeat, "Shake, shake, shake," and begin to laugh aloud. I was not privy to this inside joke; nonetheless, not wanting to feel left out, I joined in on the laughter until the day they began snickering and once again repeating, "Shake, shake, shake," while staring across the street. I turned to see what they were staring at, and to my embarrassment, it was Mami making her way down the sidewalk, shaking while she walked, just as she often did when she was inebriated. To add insult to injury, my friends had no remorse for this cruel joke. I, of course, played it off, although their laughter cut like a knife. This lack of empathy for my pain and sadness added another layer to the tough skin I was developing. Still, to this day, I unconsciously disguise my pain or hurt or uneasiness with laughter and turn negative energy into useful toughness.

* * *

My older sister, Alicia, while no longer living at home, frequently checked in on me. She made it a point to encourage me to focus on school, all the while not realizing how lost I felt. Her words of encouragement were not in vain. They would eventually resonate shortly after my why was revealed to me.

I received a letter the summer after eighth grade.

> *"To the parents of Pascual Rodriguez. Congratulations, this is your classroom and your schedule at Riverside High School."*

As might be expected, I was puzzled by this advancement, given that I missed eight months out of the eighth-grade school year. More social advancement. "Move him along; get him out" was the only justification I can think of to move me on.

I entered 9th grade with renewed enthusiasm and was intent on doing better academically. This renewed enthusiasm was short-lived when the depression and violence at home continued, coupled with the stark reality that academically I was nowhere prepared for the rigor of the high school curriculum. I reverted to what I knew best.

I started skipping school, which seemed to be an antidote to my challenges. I was getting in trouble for hanging around the school building instead of attending class. There was a nearby bike trail I would go to with some of my friends who were also skipping school. Like the saying goes, "Birds of a feather flock together." We would sneak into the school building and hang out in the bathrooms and then run away when a school official saw us.

After school, we'd casually blend in with the rest of the student body, as if we had been in attendance throughout the day. My best friend at the time, Rafael Acevedo, knew about my less-than-ideal home life, but never held that against me. I spent a lot of time with Rafael's family. They were a respectable and close-knit family. I was welcomed and eventually felt like part of the family. As an added blessing, unbeknownst to them, I would purposely make my way to their home near dinner time in anticipation of being offered a plate of food. Thankfully, they always welcomed me without question. That simple act of love nourished me both physically and emotionally, and for that, I will forever hold a special place in my heart for Rafael Acevedo, Sr. and his wife, Deyanira Acevedo.

There are some people who play a pivotal role in one's life. Rafael was that individual when I needed it most. His friendship and straight-arrow demeanor distracted me from the realities of my home life. Despite our polar-opposite circumstances, we remained close friends.

* * *

Freshman year of high school I tried out for the baseball team. I did well and made the team. Shortly thereafter the coach notified me that I was being placed on the varsity team, stating, "You have a very good skill set." Naturally I was elated at this amazing news. I felt like things were turning around, I had found a new purpose. A few days later, the coach pulled me aside and informed me that I didn't have the grades to remain eligible to play. Deflated and once again experiencing rejection, my self-esteem worsened.

The following year, I was passed on as a sophomore, with a GPA of .05. Several months into the school year, I decided to turn over a new leaf after skipping classes most of the first and second quarter. I went to my homebase and sat down. The teacher took attendance, but somehow failed to call my name. I walked up to her desk and said, "You didn't call my name." She looked at my printed schedule and then at her roster. I was instructed to go to the office where I was told, "You've been waived."

I said, "Waived, what?"

"You've been kicked out. MPS dropped you."

The next thing I knew, I was taking one of my longest walks home. Stunned and feeling completely alone, my mind replayed the phrase like a broken record, *You've been kicked out.* I thought, *Where do I go now?* I had no clue what I was going to do.

Once home, I hesitantly told Mami what had occurred. She didn't understand what was going on. I told her I had to go to Central Office to be reinstated, so off to Central Office we went. The person at the front desk looked at me and said, "Okay, we will re-enroll you, but if you miss one more day of school, you are out again. We are not playing these games." I knew that was an expectation I likely couldn't live up to.

I asked if I had other options and was told I could get my GED.

"What's that?"

The receptionist explained that a GED is an equivalency diploma, which would take several months to achieve.

I looked at Mami and told her that's what I wanted to do. I did the research and signed myself up. Six months later, I had my GED.

I'm certain there were, as is true today, teachers and administrators who took a personal approach with their students and contributed to their success. Unfortunately, I did not know them when I needed them most.

Today I have the privilege of knowing educators who are passionate about their jobs and care for their students as if they were their own children—teaching not only the ABCs, but the resilience skills to overcome challenges life throws their way!

I choose education as my profession to join the ranks of the many who are making a difference each and every day.

Reflections

- It's not the number of physical or emotional blows we receive in our lifetime, but living in the "knowing" that, as certain as the sun will rise, so will you! I needed someone to say, "I know you can do this."

- Students who have experienced multiple or chronic and prolonged developmentally adverse traumatic events often operate in a survival-in-the-moment mode and they can turn to fight, flee, or freeze modes. Have you experienced this with some students? How did/do you respond?

My biological father, Palin Rodriguez, and me.

INNING 6

"NO HIT HER"

*"Life isn't about waiting for the storm to pass.
It's about learning how to dance in the rain."*
— Vivian Greene

More often than not, when we find ourselves in the midst of a personal storm, we struggle to see the light and calmness that follows. In typical fashion, we choose to remain in the space between two opposing forces—storm and calmness—with the storm often overtaking any sense of tranquility we possess. For the luckiest among us, life has taught us that with every storm, there is a silver lining.

People often comment to me, "You must have had great parents." The assumption that my parents provided an atmosphere that promoted value in education and love for family has been rather perplexing. The old adage of "never judge a book by its cover" couldn't be any truer in this scenario. People are making the assumption that my graduating from Marquette University with my undergrad degree, and shortly thereafter, attending graduate school at National-Louis University, where I received my degree in Administrative Leadership, could only have been accomplished by coming from a family defined by "great parents."

Personally, I find this assumption rather shortsighted. My response is always, "Yeah, my parents taught me everything there is about life: the importance of education and serving as a loving husband and father."

Little do they know I succeeded by doing exactly the opposite of what my parents had done. I realized early on that my parents' way wasn't how life was supposed to be and I made a conscious decision to do the opposite. *How will I do things differently? How can I be much better than this? How can I establish a sense of "Identity Change" that was transformative and therapeutic; that was empowering?*

The theory of Identity Change suggests that, "...successful adaptation and adjustment to stressors often requires social identity change" (Drevitch, G., 2021). Basically, I needed to see myself not as a product of my environment, but a product of my choices, giving myself the power to choose my own destiny.

As a teenager, I promised myself, *I will never abuse alcohol. I will never lay a hand on my wife. I will never abandon my kids. I will always live a life, as best I can, full of integrity.*

By no means am I without fault. I am a human with imperfections, like most people. However, in most cases, I recognize my mistakes and take action to correct, improve, and move on. I chose to follow the words of Martin Luther King, *"We must accept finite disappointment, but we never lose infinite hope"* (King, February, 1968).

Believing I was going to overcome those unmanageable desolate junctures in life wasn't enough. It was HOPE—always seeking the silver lining—that sustained my resolve to lead my life rather than accept what was offered. It is through the lens of experience that I have come to this conclusion: a person is not solely the product of his or her environment, but is more importantly, a product of individual choices. YOU choose what you want to get out of life. Life is not dictated by what's around you, but by what's within you. *"Your life does not get better by chance, it gets better by change"* (Rohn, J.). Winston Churchill stated, *"To improve is to change; to be perfect is to change often."*

I have lived by these premises for most of my adult life. In order for me to become the person I desired to be, I needed to "change" the course of family history patterns that perpetuated undesirable idiosyncrasies and lifestyles.

The process of change begins by first knowing yourself. If you are true to that process, you will discover the truth, and the truth should evoke change that will lead you to personal character alignment.

These were concepts Mami could not comprehend. Her deep, undiagnosed depression and loneliness (I can only speculate) fogged her mindset, not allowing for her to recognize that change needed to occur for personal character alignment. Mami was lost in her pain and suffering and we did not have the wherewithal, the understanding, or the knowledge of how to navigate through this endless storm. As a result, our mother was there physically, but lost emotionally. Together, we existed as children and as a parent, but not as a family.

In a desperate move to feel accepted and loved, Mami met the man who would test our family's fortitude in unimaginable ways. Our home, over the next several years, would endure a tsunami of relentless assaults on the already tattered fabric of love, compassion, and safety that imperceptibly held our family intact.

His name was Sammy. Samuel Martinez. He too was an alcoholic. His drinking was accompanied with an abhorrent violent temper.

Sammy came into our lives shortly after Papi left and was present until I was an adult.

Gradually, I started seeing him more often, hanging around the house. He and Mami spent considerable time together, both day and night.

I wondered who he was. For those who have gone through parental separation and/or divorce, you understand what I'm talking about. It was a distressing experience to see another man take Papi's place in our home. Discouraging as it may have been, Sammy was in our lives, and there was little I could do to change that reality.

My uneasiness was quickly elevated when I woke up one morning to find him still there. It was the first time Sammy had spent the night, and over a short period of time, his presence became constant.

Undoubtedly, there were issues in Sammy's marriage and, within a short span of time, he was living in our home. Like most relationships, in the beginning, there is the honeymoon stage. This stage was short-lived in their relationship. After several weeks of this new living arrangement, I began witnessing another side of him.

Oddly, Mami began wearing sunglasses in the house. This oddity did not go unnoticed. She also wore long-sleeved shirts and scarves even when it was hot outdoors. To justify her choice of clothing, she would say she fell or blame it on something that was unrelated to the bruises she was covering up.

There was something happening, however, that Dalila and I couldn't quite pinpoint at the time. Initially, we were too young to engage or intervene. Later, we discovered she was covering up the marks and bruises from Sammy's physical abuse. Her arms were bruised. Eyelids and cheeks swollen. The physical abuse persisted from the time I was 11 until I was 19 years old.

As I got older, on many occasions, I found myself jumping in front of Mami before Sammy furiously made his way toward her.

In a fit of rage; he would threaten to hit her with a chair or a 2 x 4. Instinctively, I felt my only option was to intervene by physically putting myself in harm's way to block him from striking her. "No, don't hit her!" This behavior only increased his fury, resulting in a verbal tirade. Relentlessly, he would scream, yell, swear, and belittle Mami by calling her names. The following day, all would be forgiven, until the next inevitable cycle would begin.

His abusive temperament was triggered by two factors: jealousy and drunkenness. Sammy was an extremely jealous man. If Mami so much as said hello to another man, even if he was a family friend, there would be suffering and hell to pay. Sammy's despotic nature was also triggered by alcohol. He was paradoxically an individual who transformed from a kind and caring man when sober, to a severely insolent demon when intoxicated.

Incongruously, through all the physical and emotional intoxicated rants, Sammy never once laid a hand on me. I feared that his reluctance to project his rage on me may have fueled his enmity and increased his hostility toward Mami during their conflicts. I don't know why, yet I am grateful he chose not to include me in this physical abuse.

Because of this, I felt overly protective of Mami. This urge of protecting would weave itself into the fabric of my life. Today, as a husband and father, I instinctively feel a need to overly safeguard my wife and children. With that being said, when out in public, I frequently feel on guard. Call it "protective instincts." The need to ensure my wife and kids' safety is not in any way compromised. Having a visual of them is my way of establishing the trust and confidence in them that I am there. As inexplicable as this is, perhaps it's an action or habit born out of those experiences with Mami and Sammy.

* * *

My eldest sister, Alicia, was attending Parkside University, studying nursing.

It was during this time Dalila became pregnant at an early age. She moved in with her boyfriend shortly after my niece's birth.

With both of my sisters gone from the house, I was left to struggle through the pressure of Mami's increasing levels of depression and anxiety.

My sisters, along with other family members, tried to convince Mami of the danger Sammy presented. Their pleading fell on deaf ears. When all hope was lost, opportunity presented itself the night Sammy's rage cost him his freedom.

As was customary, Mami and Sammy frequented local bars throughout the week. This particular night, while intoxicated, Sammy had an altercation with a man. In the heat of the argument, Sammy pulled out a switchblade and slashed the man's face. Sammy was soon arrested and sentenced to two years in prison for assault with a deadly weapon.

Here was our opportunity to escape.

* * *

"Tipping point" is defined as, "A point at which a series of small changes or incidents become significant enough to cause a larger, more important change" (*Oxford English Dictionary*, 2018). For years, I had endured being placed somewhere toward the bottom of Mami's totem pole of priorities. My tipping point was reached when Mami chose beer over me, then demanded that I leave.

Mami's drink of choice was Pabst Blue Ribbon beer, a brand of beer that today triggers a flood of emotions within me. While our refrigerator lacked food, it was sure to be stocked with beer.

This unhealthy alcohol use came to a head one morning. I woke up, ready to eat breakfast. Instead of food, I found a six-pack of Pabst Blue Ribbon beer sitting on the refrigerator shelf. Hungry, angered, and frustrated, I grabbed the six-pack and headed toward the door to dispose of the cans. Mami demanded the beers as she lunged toward my hand, which held her desired cans.

As I held her back with my other hand, I challenged her to pick me or the beer. Without hesitation, she told me to pack my bags. In a moment of shock and disbelief, I flung the six-pack onto the street. Like Mami's history of emotional eruptions, the cans exploded. The irony of it all, like the beer cans, I found myself in the middle of the street with my belongings. My sister, Dalila, graciously opened her home to me. I was around 15 years old.

For many years thereafter, we associated alcohol as the root of the demise of our family. In reality, it was human behavior and not beer that contributed to our mother's emotional, physical, and parental decline. Still, beer is a beverage I've chosen not to drink.

A year passed while I was living with Dalila. Then I decided to reestablish my relationship with my biological father and shortly thereafter, I moved in with him. A few months later, he told me, "Uh, this isn't working out. You have to go back and live with your mom." Like a ping-pong ball never having a home on either side of the table, I felt that too familiar feeling of emotional homelessness. Papi's decision to (let's call it what it was) kick me out, was solely based on my interrupting his independence. He wanted his single lifestyle back. I was a hindrance.

Not having many options, I again packed my bags and went back to live with Mami. Although she welcomed me back, I knew what I was returning to: a dysfunctional environment to which I had sadly grown accustomed.

Sammy completed his prison sentence and returned to our home, where Mami welcomed him back. I hoped his time in prison had provided him the opportunity for reflection and sobriety, hence creating a changed man. My naivete was quickly erased when the drinking not only resumed, but it was as if they both were making up for lost time. The drinking binges intensified tenfold, and, with that, the physical abuse increased.

I spent as little time at home as possible over the next few years. When I wasn't working, I spent my free time at my girlfriend Caroline's house. I was emotionally rejected at home, but welcomed by Caroline. She filled that empty space with care and love.

* * *

It was not uncommon to see both Mami and Sammy passed out on the couch in the morning after a night of drinking. However, one particular morning in 1985, when I was 18 years old, I woke up early to head off to work at a local gas station. Mami was asleep, lying on the floor in the living room area, while Sammy was sprawled out on the couch. As usual, I navigated around their drunken bodies as I headed for the front door.

Much later that day, when I returned home from work, I noticed Mami was still sleeping, but on the couch as opposed to the floor where I had last seen her. As I often did, I said, "*Bendicion, Mami.*" She did not reciprocate my request for her blessings, which was out of character. Once again, I requested her blessings. "*Bendicion Mami.*" No response.

I asked Sammy, who was seated by the window drinking a beer, "*¿Que le pasa a Mami?* What is wrong with Mami?"

As I approached her, Sammy said, "She's been sleeping all day. I couldn't wake her up."

"How did she end up on the couch?"

"I picked her up and laid her there," Sammy stated.

"No Hit Her"

I sat next to her and called out her name. No response. I slapped her across the face to elicit a reaction, to no avail. The slap did nothing. Mami lay motionless on the couch.

I immediately called 911. When the fire department and paramedics arrived, within minutes, Mami was placed on a gurney and immediately transported to the local hospital.

Given that Mami had attempted suicide many times, we assumed she had taken pills again. Mami was initially treated as an overdose patient. When we were notified that overdose was ruled out, we suspected Sammy had played a role.

Alicia was called at 2am the following morning to inform her that a CT scan was being ordered. We anxiously awaited notice of Mami's condition.

Several hours passed before my sisters and I, along with Mami's physicians, gathered together in a private room where they proceeded to inform us, "Your mother has a massive blood clot in her brain." She would need immediate surgery. Naturally, we were stunned and wondered what had happened.

After successfully removing the clot, the medical team once again directed us to a private room. Anticipating an update on her condition, we instead received news that brought shivers down our spines.

While shaving Mami's head in preparation for the operation, the surgeon discovered an indentation on the back of her head, the size and circumference of (yes) an aluminum can. In addition, they discovered a gash on her back that was healing. It ran from the top of her neck all the way down to her buttocks. A knife wound.

Sammy later admitted to striking her on the head with a full can of beer before she had slipped into the coma. When confronted, he also admitted to causing the wound on her back.

There was a deafening silence as we tried to process what we just heard. Eventually anger and sadness filled the room. We knew Mami had a long road to recovery, and it would be up to the three of us to help her through it.

When the surgery was complete and we knew Mami was stable for the time being, I drove back to the house and asked Caroline to remain in the car. Entering my family's apartment, I saw that Sammy was seated near the window drinking a beer. I pulled up a chair and sat down positioning myself to be able to look at him face to face. He didn't say a word.

I began by saying, "You struck Mami with a beer can on her head. That's why she didn't wake up. You struck her so hard she went into a coma. I've been tolerating this kind of behavior for years. I am going to take Caroline home now. It will take me five to ten minutes to get there and the same to get back. I'll be back here in about 15 minutes."

I finished by saying, "If you're still here when I get back, I'm going to kill you. I'll go to prison today, but I don't care. I am going to kill you for all the things you have put Mami through. Today you will die. I'm giving you an opportunity to leave but if I get back and you're still here, you're leaving in a body bag."

I returned to my car and drove off.

I hadn't told Caroline what I said to him. I told her, "I'm dropping you off and I'm going back home." She knew I was angry and tried in vain to stop me, but it was too late; I had reached my tipping point. Hesitantly, she exited the car and I took off. This time, however, I was the one screeching away. The ride home did nothing to alleviate my rage. I had already accepted the fact that I was going to jail, either because I had killed Sammy or because I had severely hurt him. As I approached the front door of the apartment, I felt an intense adrenaline rush as if prepared to go to battle; prepared to go to prison!

I opened the door with full intent of following through on my threat. Instead of finding Sammy still there, I found a trail of hangers, starting at the closet and ending at the door. He had gone. He packed up and took all of his belongings.

Reality quickly set in as I glimpsed at the shadow of what would have happened if he had still been there. I was thankful that he had left. In some way, I was freed from anger. I was freed from the reality I had accepted in possibly going to prison. I was freed from the one person I hated more than anyone in the world.

* * *

Mami was making progress. She eventually began responding to stimuli and awakened from her coma four days later. She awoke completely unable to remember what happened to her. My sisters and I shared the task of explaining to her what had occurred. Our narrative was very blunt, and included our concern about her drinking, but most importantly about her relationship with Sammy.

Her longing for someone to love her had handicapped her ability to view her own self-worth. She had accepted Sammy through all the torment and abuse. This acceptance defined her belief that, *This is all I'm worth. If I lose him, then I have nobody.*

Mami made a good enough recovery to be released from the hospital. After living with her sister for a little over a month, we moved her into a first-floor duplex on 18th Street and Scott Streets. During this time, Mami remained sober, and for the first time in years, lived a life free from pain, emotional neglect, and psycho-logical injustice. There was a sense of hope for her future.

Four months later, without warning and to our dismay, Sammy was back in the picture.

* * *

My sisters and I were incensed and confused at Mami's lack of discretion. How could someone who experienced a traumatic attack at the hands of a vicious and contemptuous person consider accepting him back? We could tell Mami was lonely. My sisters and I worked full-time, leaving Mami alone most of the day. She no longer lived within walking distance to visit relatives. She was companionless, thus seeking love, acceptance, and a purpose to live.

She found that purpose in Sammy.

"Today you will die!" Little did I know my words would come to fruition. A death, in fact, had occurred.

The death of evil. The death of abuse. And the death of the man I had formerly wished dead.

Sammy returned completely sober. There was a peacefulness about him. He appeared loving, supportive, and completely devoted to Mami. They were both in a state of sobriety. Normally people reach this level through counseling and treatment. Mami and Sammy, separately, had decided to stop drinking and, when reunited, kept that sobriety going.

Although at first skeptical, I felt the house was full of a kind of peace and humility that had been lacking for so long. They spent every waking hour together; inseparable, and enjoyed each other's company. Sammy did the majority of the cooking, as well as the household chores. My sisters and I ultimately forgave him, never mentioning his past transgressions. Seeds of trust were planted and began to blossom.

Later, Mami and Sammy would care for our children when Caroline and I were working. Sammy became part of the family. He was devoted to Mami and loved and cared for her until his dying day.

All in all, I witnessed a man transform from someone I wished dead (someone I could have killed) to someone who, I can completely say, I loved. In the eyes of my children, Sammy was their grandfather, Papa. Although very young, they wept and felt a void when he passed away. On the contrary, when my father, their biological grandfather, passed away, my children did not shed a tear. By my father's choice, they did not have a relationship with him. Needless to say, neither did I.

* * *

Long after Mami and Sammy stopped drinking, the effects of alcohol abuse took tolls on their bodies. Ironically, both ended up needing, and having, liver transplants.

During the spring of 1992, Mami became critically ill and was informed she had three weeks to live. She was 52 years old. Her liver had failed and other organs were affected as well. She was forced to face the consequences of alcohol abuse. Before this inevitable outcome, Mami became a woman of faith. She devoted her time and energy to serving the Lord through her local Pentecostal church. It was her faith in God that she clung to during this critical time. I remember thinking how unfair this predicament was. Everything Mami endured, all the shortcomings and misdeeds done against her, and this was how her life would end?

During her hospitalization, she called me to her bedside and said she had come to the realization that she was going to die. She told me she didn't have much, just a bank account with $200 in it. She wanted me to keep it. I was completely stunned. How was it that on her supposed death bed, her only concern was my well-being? It was truly one of the most emotional moments between us. Against all odds, I maintained my prayer and hope.

She was placed on the liver transplant wait list. Shortly thereafter, sadly, but to Mami's benefit, a nine-year-old Brookfield boy died on May 24 when he was struck by a car while riding his bike. His parents generously donated his organs. We received the call that Mami would gain his liver. The operation took place on my 26th birthday. As expected, she went through an initial rejection phase like some transplant recipients do. With treatment she recuperated and lived an additional 18 years.

Months later, we received an anonymous letter from the boy's parents. They stated that they hoped their son had not died in vain and that his organ recipients would live lives of integrity. They chose not to know who received the organs. It wasn't out of lack of respect. It was the painful memory of their son that kept them from meeting the recipients. Their pain inadvertently became our joy and thanksgiving. That young boy and Mami would forever be connected. I believe he was Mami's angel. He gave Mami a second chance—a chance to hold and enjoy her grandchildren and great-grandchildren—the absolute loves of her life.

On October 10th, 2010, seventy-one years after she entered into this world, Mami passed away, freed from her decrepit body and as I can imagine gracefully joined with that little boy in heaven as they held hands and for the first time together, joyfully danced.

Following Mami's successful transplant, Sammy was diagnosed with liver failure several years later. He was placed on the transplant wait list and eventually received a liver. The donor was a 60-year-old individual. Unfortunately, within a five-year span, Sammy's body rejected the liver, and he went back on the wait list for a second transplant. Although the second transplant was believed to have a better prognosis, Sammy continued to experience intermittent complications, which eventually worsened. On July 5th, 2005, with our family by his bedside, Sammy succumbed to complications of liver failure and peacefully passed away.

The image of Mami lunging onto Sammy's body as he flatlined will be ingrained in my memory forever. She yelled out loudly, "*No te valles*. Don't leave." Mami was completely heartbroken. A little piece of her died with him.

Both Mami and Sammy several years after their liver transplants holding newly born grandchild, Joseph Decker (2000).

Reflections

- Forgiveness is the ability to open up the doors of hope and set your soul free. Have you ever experienced this?

- Respect can be earned through changed behavior. As an educator, how do you develop respect and trust in your classroom?

INNING 7

A Cross, A Rose, A Ring, and Yes, A Grand Slam

Given the lack of family structure in my late teens, I longed for emotional connection and eventually found it break dancing with the Magic Rockers. They immediately became my surrogate family and break dancing filled a void lacking from my home life. I mention this because this group not only took me away from my home reality, they also introduced me to the one person who would change my life forever.

I loved break dancing! The exhilarating feeling I got from spinning on my back, spinning on my head, and generating and contorting my body in a gymnastic sort of way was exciting. Yet, it wasn't until years later that I realized all the incredible moves, cheers from spectators as we performed in various venues across the state of Wisconsin, and the Midwest weren't what I loved most. It was the love and acceptance of a group of guys who filled the void in my life. Family.

There were 16 members of the Magic Rockers, and we bonded like brothers. We spent time together practicing, traveling, and performing. We celebrated our birthdays like a family, we grieved together during moments of sadness, and like most brothers, we argued over frivolous matters, embarrassed one another, yet forgave and resumed our brotherhood.

This ostensibly family-orientated group of guys remained together for close to two years, and as quickly as the art of breakdancing infiltrated our curiosity and pop culture, those two years seemed to fly by. Before I knew it, that era faded away and so did our brother-hood.

It was during this time that I met Caroline. She was a member of the Latin Dolls Break Dance group.

* * *

We originally met at a local community center, during a taping of a Milwaukee morning talk show featuring an episode on the break dance craze. Several break dance groups were asked to illustrate moves, including the Magic Rockers and the Latin Dolls.

Pascual and Caroline (1990).

Caroline was asked to show the host how to perform a back spin. She eagerly sat next to him on the floor, and explained how to simultaneously lie on your back on the floor while whipping your leg around your body in a spinning motion. Not realizing how close she was sitting next to the host, she inadvertently kicked him in the head, nearly knocking him out. Luckily, he took the incident in stride and kept it in the show as a blooper.

I was definitely attracted to her. We spoke briefly and there was an obvious interest on both sides. She gave me her phone number and we parted ways. For some reason, I didn't call her for the next several months.

One night, I randomly decided to call her. We spent the next five to six hours on the phone. I can't remember what we talked about—just life and who we were. We went out on a couple of dates and shortly thereafter while at a bus stop—our only means of transportation at the time—I turned to her and asked, "Do you want to be my lady?" Admittedly, a corny way of asking a girl out, but it worked. She said, "Sure." We were both 17 years old. We dated mostly steadily for the next seven years.

I met Caroline at the height of my challenges with Mami and didn't take her to my house for months because of the circumstances at home. In fact, house is an understatement because we were living in a converted store made into a small apartment. When I finally had the guts to take Caroline home to meet Mami, she could see Mami was intoxicated, but greeted her nonetheless. She didn't seem bothered by the lack of furniture and unkept surroundings. She never batted an eye. Even though it was not a traditional house, Caroline made herself at home, which immediately put me at ease.

Caroline and I had dated for about a year before that fateful day when Sammy struck Mami over the head. During that difficult time, she was supportive and was that ray of hope for me to see how things could be as I removed myself from my reality and entered some other fantasy with her.

On April 1, 1984, I asked Caroline to be my girlfriend. We still debate about who said "I love you" first. Her love sustained me and gave me hope for a brighter future. We celebrate that day—not an April Fool's day to us—rather, a gift of a new beginning.

* * *

During those years of dating, Caroline and I experienced lots of ups and downs in our relationship. Having a deep need to feel wanted, I became attached to her and admittedly held on tightly.

Rejection was, and still is, something I struggle with. I came to believe that it is a byproduct of being rejected by my father, rejected by my mother, rejected by school officials, and in some sense, rejected by professional baseball. It is the one notion I struggle with the most. Throughout my life, I have found myself seeking approval from others. Lack of affirmation made me question my worth. Before Caroline and I were married, every argument and break-up reinforced that feeling of rejection.

There were also definite trust and abandonment issues on my end. Jealousy caused a major wedge between us for several years. Caroline was a social butterfly. She reveled in her teenage friendships and liked to have fun. Although just friends, I couldn't help but feel jealous and angry when she spoke to another guy. Each time we argued and she wanted to end the relationship, I found myself begging her to take me back. I would find myself apologizing even when I was not at fault to re-establish peace between us. It was an unhealthy foundation where I eventually realized I was short-changing myself. I realized I was the one putting forth the most effort to keep this relationship going.

One day, I decided I'd had enough and wanted to end our relationship, which devastated her, but I had made my decision and stuck to it. I stopped caring about the silly arguments and as fate would have it, she became the one who began needing me. A classic pendulum shift. We had been separated for three or four months when I found myself spiraling—just not caring about life. It reached a pinnacle point the day I defended a friend who was ready to fight a mutual acquaintance. Being the protector, I turned the attention to myself, and before I knew it, we were brawling. I immediately realized my life was out of control.

I jumped on my bike to ride to the one person who brought purpose to my life. I rode to Caroline's house. She was shocked to see me at her front door, but welcomed me nonetheless. We sat on the front porch as I shared with her what had just transpired, and how I had been feeling since we broke up. We gradually began speaking more often and eventually got back together, making it a point to mend our relationship.

One of Caroline's most attractive attributes for me was her religious faith. She was a practicing Catholic. It was a structure I lacked. She invited me to attend church with her at St Patrick's Parish located on Milwaukee's south side. I loved the cultural Latino choir with its tropical beat.

In addition, we were asked to join the newly formed youth group named Youth for Jesus. We met every Saturday night from 7 to 9. On Wednesdays, we gathered together to plan Saturday night's schedule, which included skits, music, and religious speeches from out-of-town guests or older parish members. On any given Saturday night, there would be anywhere from 50 to 60 youth in attendance.

It was a time when most of the people our age were out partying at nightclubs. We, on the other hand, were in a church setting, in service to God, volunteering our time to youth. I took a liking to working with kids and discovered I was making a difference in some of their lives, especially the young boys who were struggling through life due to an absentee father or an alcoholic or drug-addicted parent, and who may have otherwise been overlooked. I was able to reach some by sharing my story, thus giving them some sense of hope.

After Caroline and I were married, we volunteered with the youth group until our first child was born. While working with St. Patrick's youth group, Caroline and I didn't realize at the time that we were building a concrete foundation that would stand the test of time.

* * *

How had I proposed to Caroline?

It wouldn't have been possible or turned out as perfectly if it wasn't for our dear friends Marilu and Ruben Rivera. It was a beautiful Sunday afternoon and the plan was in motion. Marilu and Ruben had been married the year prior and they were more than eager to help me pull off my secretive proposal.

The chosen place for this elaborate scheme was Schoenstatt, a Catholic retreat center that offers spiritual renewal and focuses on family formation. Located in Waukesha, Schoenstatt is a peaceful and transformational place, surrounded by nature, trails, and a prayer-filled atmosphere. Caroline had spent time there as a child with her family and later we attended youth conferences and retreats there together.

Along one of the trails is a large wooden cross where people often went to reflect and pray. It was the perfect place for the proposal.

I bought a dozen roses and gave them to Marilu, along with the engagement ring. The plan was that Marilu would announce that she and Ruben wanted to spend some time alone and we would catch up with them later.

When the time came, they took the quickest route to the cross, where they hurriedly spread the rose petals around it, except for one rose that was placed behind the cross. Marilu stationed the engagement ring in the center of that rose. Then they hid in the nearby cornstalks on the lookout to make sure no one came and disrupted things.

When we reached the cross, Caroline said, "Look, someone spread rose petals. How beautiful," not knowing the surprise awaiting her.

Offering roses to Blessed Mother Mary is a Catholic tradition, so I knew my plan was solid. We made ourselves comfortable and when she closed her eyes to breathe in the sweet sun-filled air, I knelt down, reached around the cross, and took hold of the rose. When she opened her eyes and saw the ring on top of the rose, she immediately began crying. I prayed they were tears of joy.

"Would you marry me?"

Her response was a joyful and tearful, "Yes."

Sadly Marilu and Ruben were too far away to be able to take pictures, but the memory remains engraved in our hearts.

It was important that the proposal was something faith-based because the church and faith are both meaningful to her. We were married August 3, 1991, and a little after our first year anniversary, we welcomed our first child, Pascual Angel Rodriguez Jr. We were officially a family. Pascual's birth was followed by Andrew, Monica and finally, to complete the

Our wedding day, August 3, 1991.

grand slam, Emilie blessed our lives. My marriage and children have been my greatest blessings. I owe my entire happiness to them. Not a day goes by that I don't thank God for this precious gift.

* * *

Before we married, Caroline had decided to go to college. At that point, I was still trying to figure out my *"why"* after being released from the California Angels.

What is my purpose now, if it isn't baseball? I asked myself,

89

I knew I enjoyed working with kids from our work with Youth for Jesus, but I didn't know in what capacity.

Caroline decided to go to Milwaukee Area Technical College (MATC) and asked me to join her for a visit to the college. I went along with no intention of signing up for classes. As we walked the halls of the technical college, I heard someone say, "Pascual, Pascual!"

I immediately turned around to see who was trying to get my attention. It was one of my previous volleyball teammates, Dr. Wilma Bonaparte. I hadn't known she was the Director of the Educational Program. She said, "Pascual, I have something to offer you. How would you like to make $325 a month?" She went on to say that she was going to pay for my tuition and school supplies through a grant called CUTEP (Cooperative Urban Teacher Education Program). That got my attention.

I said, "You want to pay me to go to school? Sure, why not."

It would be years later before I would come to realize the impact that conversation would have on the trajectory of my life.

I spent the next two years taking prerequisite classes along with pre-education courses in preparation to transfer to a four-year university. Prior to starting the program, I took a placement test and scored low on the math portion. I was obligated to take a basic math course. However, as I expected, I excelled rather quickly and soon started building my math comprehension and became the top student. Within those two years, my math skills and comprehension were recognized by my instructors and I was eventually asked to be a math tutor in the math lab. As promised, everything was paid for.

Holding down a full-time job, being married and a new father, and full-time student, I made it through the two years at MATC. I was ready to transfer and move onward to my next step. My options were Marquette University or University of Wisconsin-Madison. Because we had started our family, the choice was easy. Marquette University, located in Milwaukee.

Between Milwaukee Area Technical College and Marquette University, it took me nearly seven years to complete my undergraduate degree. Although there were obstacles along the way, I learned I could make up for my academic shortcomings by applying myself. Before I knew it, I was holding my own.

This endeavor, however, came with a price. I wasn't your typical student. My obligations as husband and father required me to forgo the liveliness of college life. While most students hung around campus, local bars and pubs enjoying carefree time outside of the classroom, I was hustling to class after an eight-hour workday with Milwaukee Public Schools (MPS)—School to Work Transition Program—then home or the library to study.

Not much time was left for Caroline and our children. Caroline understood the sacrifice it would take to achieve my academic goals, so she did the best she could holding down the fort, while I was being pulled in different directions. There were days I left the house in the early morning and did not return home until after the kids were in bed asleep.

Thankfully, Fridays were my lighter days. I was scheduled for one or two classes, allowing me to come home early. Missing out on playtime with my children, missing some milestones, and not spending enough quality time was painful to say the least. Sometimes my only moments with my children were when they woke up during the night for feedings, thus giving Caroline the chance to rest.

With that being said, I felt I needed to stay focused on my ultimate goal for the betterment of my family. Although I missed out on a lot, it was a necessary sacrifice and personal goal I set for myself. I was able to push through it by setting a timetable goal. I told myself, "I'm going to be 31 with or without a degree."

Thirty-one was the magic number. Every time I felt like giving up, I reminded myself of that goal. The thought of turning 31 and not having a degree felt as if I would be failing myself and failing my family. You can't stop aging, but you can change the path of your life during that process.

I had never been able to walk across a graduation stage, so the prospect of this upcoming first-time event felt surreal. I could almost feel the diploma in my hands. What made the thought sweeter was the fact that my wife, children, and family would be in attendance.

My dream finally came true in December of 1997 when I obtained my B.A. in sociology/secondary education. However, the experience of walking across the stage to receive a diploma was still an unmet goal, given that Marquette University under-graduates were asked to stand when their name was called, instead of walking across the stage.

My sister Alicia had been the first in our family to graduate from college and I followed thereafter. By then, I was more than ready to move onto my next educational ambition. I began my master's program in the summer of 1998 through National-Louis University. The main campus is located in Illinois, but the school also has a Wisconsin site. The demand was not as intense as undergrad. Class met every Wednesday night, allowing me to make up for lost time with my family. I finished my master's in May, 2000. Finally, the moment that had eluded me in high school and at my undergrad graduation came to fruition. There I stood at the footsteps of a lifelong pursuit of crossing the stage as I received a diploma. However, I did not cross that stage alone. Accompanying me in that compelling moment were those individuals who played significant roles in that accomplishment: my wife, my children, my mother, my sisters, Dr Bonaparte, and the grace of God.

Most importantly, without the support of Caroline and her inspiration to keep going, I'm not sure I would have finished. Along with that, having a purpose and motivation to provide for my family was the catalyst that kept my eye on the prize—a college diploma.

Reflections

- I learned that, although I had some flaws and lacked academic support, I still had the potential for greatness. Having supporters made all the difference. How do you support striving for greatness among students?

- Walking across that stage proved to me that my choices would determine my destiny, not my circumstances. How can educators convey this reality to students?

Our children on a vacation day in Florida 2002:
Bottom Right - Pascual Angel Jr.
Bottom Left - Andrew Michael
Top Left - Monica Maria
Top RIght - Emilie Rose.

Celebrating our son, Pascual Jr.'s, wedding day August 28, 2020.

Pascual Jr. and Colleen Rodriquez. Post-COVID-19 wedding celebration, August 28, 2021.

INNING 8

Sweet Spot: My *"WHY"*

Over the last seven innings, I have shared moments of joy, laughter, and sadness. All of it was designed to establish my *why* and what I have chosen to do with that knowledge. As I reflect and allow myself to become vulnerable, unleashing memories hidden deep within my consciousness, I do so with one single objective, which is to inspire and motivate you, the reader, to search and discover your *why*, but more importantly, what to do with it.

As for me, my *why* has led me to reflect on how I can and have impacted the lives of students through my work as an educator. Over my 25+ year career as both teacher and principal, I have come to the conclusion that the souls of children (their innocence) are more important than their cognitive ability or their intelligence.

I believe educators, business owners, and supervisors need to be attuned to the social and emotional lives of their students/ employees. Although this concept can be utilized by multiple professional disciplines, I will focus my attention on the profession I have come to love and admire: education.

The following is the current culmination of ideas that have emerged from my life experiences and knowledge as an educator: **T.R.A.A.C.K. to IMPACT**. Before I discuss my six universal traits to ensure students' social and emotional well-being, let me share with you one of my greatest moments as an educator in my

97

25-year career. This story will provide a framework for **T.R.A.A.C.K. to IMPACT** and can serve as a guide for how you might implement it in your own teaching and life.

My first teaching job was at Milwaukee's Bay View High School. During one morning's prep time, as I was leaving my classroom and making my way to the office, I noticed a young lady walking the hall toward my classroom. This was not the first time I had seen this freshman meandering the hallways, seemingly uninterested in attending class.

As fate would have it, our paths crossed at that decisive moment. Seeing her reminded me of how I had felt my freshman year in high school. I flashed back to my emotions after being passed on to ninth grade, even though I had missed eight months of school the previous year. It was as if I was insignificant to everyone, and my absences did not resonate with anyone in the school. I lacked the feeling of belonging to a class. It was because the failure of educating my mind was directly attributed to the failure of reaching my heart.

Something—call it intuition—prompted me to ask this young lady, "May I speak with you?" She looked perplexed but acceded to my request. I recall making our way back to my classroom and asking her to have a seat. It turned out (like me) she had a troubled background. She was disengaged and continuously found herself being kicked out of class and on the suspension list. This was a common occurrence I could relate to from my own high school days.

In his book, *Even on Your Worst Day, YOU CAN BE A STUDENT'S BEST HOPE*, Manny Scott writes, "We cannot solve all our students' problems, but we can work hard to open their eyes and help them see themselves in a different light" (Scott 2017). Scott was referring to a teacher's ability to influence a student's self-concept.

What was this young lady's reality? Had anyone ever sat her down, with care and compassion, and asked her, "What is going on with you?" rather than, "What is wrong with you?"

Did she know her self-worth? Was there trauma she had experienced that influenced and hindered her ability to function as a student?

I would have welcomed someone asking me what was going on when I was going through my ordeal as a teen and a student, and now I was damned if I was going to take a pass with this young lady to redeem my personal promise to intervene when moved to do so. So, I did. I asked her, "What is going on with you?"

For the next 20 or 30 minutes, we talked, or should I say, I did most of the talking, while she did the listening. I shared a brief testimony on my life and the changes I would make if given the opportunity to push the reset button. In addition, I encouraged her to acknowledge the reality of the destructive and self-sabotaging behaviors impacting her social and academic progress. In that moment, I attempted to convince her that the future was her choice. My hope was that she could see that her current reality did not have to determine her destiny, but the choices she made moving forward would.

During our time together, I had the impression, by her slouching, non-interested body language, that I was wasting her time. At the end, I asked if she had anything to say, and as with most disconnected youth, I got a shrug of the shoulders followed by a, "No." I thanked her for her time and wished her the best of luck.

She rose from the chair and walked out. I never saw her again. Naturally, I questioned my tactics and wondered if my words had fallen on deaf ears. Did my attempt to influence her self-concept fail? I battled over those questions for days, and reflected on those moments, asking myself, "What could I have done or said differently?"

Ironically, those questions would be answered three years later. NOTHING! Do nothing differently.

Another school year was ending when I received a card. I immediately thought someone was sending me birthday wishes. However, it was not a birthday card—it was a thank you card.

At that moment, I could not think of anything I had done to merit a thank you, but to my astonishment, it turned out to be a card from that young lady.

Allow me to paraphrase her words.

> *Dear Mr. Rodriguez, you may not remember me, but I will never forget you! I was the young lady you pulled into your classroom and asked to have a seat. You proceeded to tell me about your story, and where you saw me headed if I continued down a destructive path. You may have thought I wasn't listening, but I was. No one had ever taken the time to speak to me the way you did, and for that, I am thankful.*
>
> *That evening, I sobbed as your words resonated within my mind, but most importantly, within my heart. That night, I decided to change the pathway of my destiny and take full responsibility for my choices.*
>
> *In the next couple of weeks, I will be graduating from high school with honors and will attend college. This would not have been possible if not for the time you took to speak with me. Thank you for being the difference in my life. Thank you for caring enough to invest time out of your day to speak to me. I will be eternally grateful!*

Reading her words, I felt as if everything I had gone through in my life was, in a way, vindicated. My experiences and willingness to risk encountering this young Latina had changed a child's path. I'll never forget that moment. In my 25 years of experience as an educator, that is the one compelling moment that helped influence how I would engage with students throughout my career. My only regret is that I don't remember her name. But she knows who I am.

I remember returning to my classroom after reading the card, attempting to fight back the tears as I sat and reflected back to when I was in her shoes and no one ever seemed to care, yet in a matter of 20 or 30 minutes, I had been able to impact a student's life. It was that emotional. That experience confirmed my *why*: why I chose education as my profession.

* * *

Recently, a Johns Hopkins research study of over 6,100 adults revealed seven Protective Childhood Experiences (PCEs) that contributed to well-being and positive mental health in adults (Braman, 2021). Research shows that even children who experienced a high score on the Adverse Childhood Experience (ACE)* were able to have normal development, as well as good mental health as adults if they had some Protective Childhood Experiences.

The seven PCEs are:
1) Ability to talk to family about feelings,
2) Felt experience that family is supportive in difficult times,
3) Enjoy participation in the community traditions,
4) Feeling of belonging in high school,
5) Feeling of being supported by friends,
6) Having at least two non-parent adults who genuinely care, and
7) Feeling safe and protected by an adult at home.

---

*See Appendix A for the ACE questions.

Perhaps the young Latina's path was impacted to some degree by PCEs #4 and #6 after our talk. Maybe she felt a deeper sense of belonging and saw that there was at least one adult who genuinely cared about her.

Given that my focus is on how educators can influence the trajectory of a child's pathway to a positive and rewarding educational experience—which in turn increases that child's level of resiliency in response to adversity—I will focus my attention on PCE's #4, #5, and #6, within the **T.R.A.A.C.K. to IMPACT** interventions because educators cannot directly influence the other four PCEs. As for the young lady, my hope is that she has paid it forward and has become a voice and emotional support for those feeling marginalized.

Reflections

- As educators, we must be intentionally aware that life experiences, rather than defiance or spitefulness, may be impacting a student's ability to concentrate or plan. Their behavior may seem unpredictable and impulsive. How do you intervene with students experiencing these kinds of life experiences?

- Sometimes self-sabotaging behavior is caused by an imbalance between emotional and logical thinking. Do you have strategies for helping students understand how they are hurting themselves and impacting their futures?

- Before the child becomes a student, they are first a human. This is a lesson for us all. You can't teach the mind until you reach the heart.

ROUNDING THIRD &
FINALLY HOME
—T.R.A.A.C.K. TO IMPACT—
SIX UNIVERSAL TRAITS TO ENSURE STUDENTS'
SOCIAL AND EMOTIONAL WELL-BEING

The six universal traits that I believe are critical to any educational experience to ensure students' social and emotional well-being both in the classroom and beyond are: **T**rust, **R**espect, **A**cknowledge, **A**ffirmation, **C**are, and **K**now (they will succeed).

In developing these traits, I assumed that social and emotional development evolves as children start to understand who they are, what they are feeling, and what to expect when interacting with others. They learn to form and sustain positive relationships. They develop the abilities to experience, manage, and express emotions.

Social and emotional development consists of three main areas of children's self-regulation in:

1) Acting: behaving in socially appropriate ways and ways that foster learning,

2) Feeling: understanding others' emotions and regulation of one's own emotions, and

3) Thinking: regulating attention and thoughts.

However, when this development is interrupted by Complex Traumatic Experiences (CTE), a child's ability to navigate through his/her challenges becomes exponentially more difficult. Wolpow addresses the impacts of Complex Traumatic Episodes in the book, *The Heart of Learning and Teaching: Compassion, Resiliency, and Academic Success* (Wolpow, 2016). Students who have experienced multiple or chronic and prolonged developmentally adverse traumatic events—most often of a personal nature (sexual or physical abuse, family violence, war, community violence)—often operate in a survival-in-the-moment mode, resulting in fight, flee, or freeze reactions.

The science of understanding the human brain is apparent when a student operates in these fight, flee, or freeze modes. We may ask whether this behavior is inherited (pre-wired) or learned (from exposure and life influences). We now know that human brain development continues into adulthood, which has implications for how we interact with children in our classrooms.

As educators, we must be intentionally aware that life experiences, rather than defiance or spitefulness, may be impacting students ability' to concentrate or plan. Their behavior may seem unpredictable and impulsive. They may exhibit personality changes. They may show self-sabotaging behaviors—imbalance between emotional and logical thinking, behaviors that were present for me as a boy going through my own traumatic experiences.

In many cases, according to the *School Climate and Safety Report* (Office of Civil Rights, U.S. Department of Education 2018), 2.7 million K-12 students were suspended at least once during the 2015-16 school year, the most recent year for which data is available. In most cases, students of color, who come from economically disadvantaged homes or lack access to meaningful resources, tend to bear the effects of traumatic experiences, which translates into behaviors that result in school disciplinary actions. The reasons students found themselves on the suspension lists varied by state, but most often included injuring, harassing, bullying, or threatening other students (including verbal, physical, sexual, and/or cyberbullying). One common theme among students who engage in self-sabotaging behavior can be caused by what I like to term as the imbalance between emotional and logical thinking.

When emotions are high, logical thinking may be low. If a child is high on the emotions side of a scale and low on logical thinking, what that is basically signaling is an interruption in the logical sequencing of the thought process. This interruption leads to behaviors that lack appropriate response to feelings and subsequently affect one's ability to act or respond in logical ways.

Behaviors present as emotional reactions vs. rational responses, and brain science supports why this happens. As Dan Siegel's research demonstrates,* students who experience trauma and chronic stress have overactive amygdalas, which causes students to be in "survival mode"—a constant state of "fight, flee, or freeze." As educators, we have learned more about the social and emotional qualities of our students over the years. In the article, "Flip Your Lid—the Effects of Trauma on a Child's Brain," Michelle Wenz writes, "There has been extensive research into the effects of trauma on the brain. Studies show there are three major parts of the brain involved in a response to trauma."

The three parts are:

1) Brain stem: Part of the brain that controls bodily functions used for survival (e.g. regulating heartbeat, lung function, and levels of arousal);

---

*Daniel J. Siegel is a clinical professor of psychiatry at the UCLA School of Medicine and executive director of the Mindsight Institute.

2) The limbic system: Responsible for emotions and relationships/attachment;

Three components of the limbic system are:

- Hypothalamus, the command center for hormones,

- Amygdala, the emotional switchboard, and

- Hippocampus, the memory maker;

3) Cortex: The outer layer of the brain, where rational thinking lives.

Basically, when all three of these components are working in unison, "logical" thinking is at its optimum. When there is a disconnect or a traumatic event, "emotions" are the prevailing driver with logical thinking either completely absent or minimally present resulting in illogical thinking or lack thereof.

When educators fail to seek the reason behind student disengagement, disruptiveness, and destructiveness in the classroom and instead respond to it only in punitive ways, a devastating and profound impact on a child's emotional, physical, and psychological well-being is likely to ensue.

If children are not emotionally present (thinking logically), they are not ready to learn.

Unfortunately, what too often happens is that, as educators, we see students come through our doors, but we fail to recognize the *human* beings. I do not mean that in a facetious way. I mean that *student* has a certain connotation. Certain assumptions. If you are a student, you are in the classroom to learn a particular content area. As a teacher, I am going to *track* your grades, *track* your attendance, *track* your behavior, *track* your homework and subsequently your assignment grades, and *track* your formative and summative assessments.

But imagine if you, as an educator, begin with the idea that the child walking through the door is much more than a student. In fact, I would challenge teachers to shift their thinking from seeing children as students to seeing them as people who seek to be loved and cared for first and taught second. I imagine what a safe haven school and my teachers could have been for me as a youth if someone had intervened on my behalf. I imagine what a difference it could have made if I had been allowed to play varsity baseball in high school and been part of a team.

As previously stated, *"You can't teach the mind until you reach the heart."* You cannot impact a student until you first make a positive personal impression on the child. For this, we need a paradigm shift in pedagogical thinking, from teacher-leads-students, to a "reflective practice" where there is an *"...internal understanding of our choices and actions through continual evaluation of the effects of these on those with whom we work,"* (Wolpow & Johnson) in this case, children.

A stressed child may experience an emotional and intellectual disconnect. His or her frustrations lead to the inability to concentrate and likely lead to *disengaged, disruptive,* and *even destructive* behavior.

Too often, this disengagement, disruptiveness, and destructiveness may be exhibited by adults (in this case, teachers) first, with reverberating consequences that have a devastating and profound impact on a child's emotional, physical, and psychological well-being.

You are not just a teacher. You are a school counselor, you are an aunt or uncle, you are a friend, you are the difference between success and failure. You empower or disempower. You recognize students' dreams or confirm their nightmares. But of all things, *loving and caring* for students is the greatest of all the compassionate pedagogical practices teachers can adhere to.

* * *

So, how can we, as educators, create this paradigm shift? Let us dive into the six universal traits for students' emotional well-being and educational success.

T.R.A.A.C.K. to IMPACT

Trust
Respect
Acknowledge
Affirm
Care
Know (they will succeed)

Clearly, none of these six words are exclusively associated with education or a student's cognitive ability to function within a school setting. Nonetheless, it's these six seemingly basic words that can make the difference between a child's social-emotional learning successes or failures. Let's delve into each one to see how they have an impact on children.

TRUST

He who does not trust enough, will not be trusted.
—Lao Tzu

What school interventions could have helped me as I navigated through turbulent times as a young preteen and teenage adolescent? The teachers did not have much control, or knowledge for that matter, over the daily hardships and volatile environment I was exposed to in my home (not to the extent where a social worker would have gotten involved).

I would have benefitted from a caring and loving adult, a caring and supportive teacher. I needed someone who saw me as much more than just a student, but a child who, through no fault of his own, lacked the compassion, understanding, support, and most of all, love of another adult. Someone who talked to me. Someone who understood why I might not have been quite prepared academically. Someone with the compassion not to seek to embarrass me by asking me questions they knew I could not answer, then toss me from class when I responded negatively, disguising my deficiencies of content knowledge through disruptive behavior. Just to be clear, as it is for most children, I never woke up in the morning saying, "I can't wait to go to school, be a jerk, and give Ms. XX a hard time."

I longed for someone to acknowledge my emotional, psychological, and physical inequities. Someone to see through my facade of toughness and trust that my behavior was nothing more than a strong cry for help. Someone to understand that, although equations, algorithms, principles of sentence syntax, and scientific hypotheses are important to the building blocks of intellectual capacities, survival was the dominant force that consumed every minute of my day. I may have been in class physically, but my mind was trapped in a world of hurt, confusion, and fear of the unknown I was going to come home to.

As a teacher, I have acknowledged my students' presence. I acknowledged that they existed as more than just students. I sometimes shared how I was raised, that my parents were divorced and how my dad left when I was eleven years old. But I did not get into deep details because I did not think that was professional or within my capacity to engage in that type of conversation.

My point to the students was you do have a choice at the end of the day. I found myself telling students, "At this minute in time, you can either choose to be disruptive, destructive, or disrespectful, or you can try to leave this classroom being a little bit better than when you came in, regardless of whatever is happening at home." I would ask the students to think and be selfish with their lives for a moment.

For some students, I could not ask for a full 50 minutes of attention, but maybe I could hold them for 30 minutes giving them a break. Take the time out for the other 20 minutes because, "I trust that you know what you're doing, what you need to do." My efforts were to bolster their self-efficacy, creating a sense of maturation, and increasing school engagement.

Trust builds and students know you are not going to ask them a question knowing full well they don't know the answer.

Students need to trust their educators. And they need to know that their teachers trust them to make the right decisions, with a little guidance. They need to know their teacher really cares—not only about the grades they assign, but also about their lives outside of the classroom and who they are as people.

RESPECT

Treat people the way you want to be treated. Talk to people the way you want to be talked to. Respect is earned, not given.
—Hussein Nishah

Trust and respect are connected. Respect is, in my mind, the most important construct teachers need to commit to in establishing a positive and effective relationship with their students. If teachers do not show a child respect, they will undoubtedly disconnect themselves from that child's reality.

The most effective teachers *earn* their students' respect, not *demand* it. That means coming in and understanding them as people. When students feel respected, certain qualities like good attendance, good behavior, and good academic skills (to the students' best ability) often follow. Feeling cared for and supported, students are empowered to do—and want to do—their best.

The young lady I singled out and talked to respected me in some ways. She was not my student, but probably had heard of me somewhere down the road, most likely through the high school chatter mill.

My first year teaching, the high school had a survey that asked the students' who their two favorite teachers were. In a school of 1,700 students, another teacher and I were named. What was the commonality? We both showed compassion towards the students. The other teacher was a woman, short in stature, with a no-nonsense attitude. She loved her students and it showed, building that foundational respect. It was an amazing thing to witness.

I taught American government/civics and world cultures. These are not easy subjects to teach. To keep the students' attention, I had to make it entertaining! Being that I have a humorous disposition, it was fairly easy to keep the students engrossed. At the first parent/teacher conference of each year, it was not uncommon to hear parents say things like, "My child didn't care for you at first but now says you're absolutely her favorite teacher." Why? In the beginning of the semester, I was notorious for classroom strictness and full attention. It was important that I establish discipline. I would begin by saying, "We will learn about democracy, we will learn what it means to practice civic responsibility; therefore we will establish what being 'civically responsible' means and transfer that knowledge and understanding to what it means to be a productive student."

I was stern and had high expectations for ALL students; regardless of their backgrounds or the reputations they may have established over the years. However, once I got their attention and they understood their boundaries, I softened up a little bit and became very interactive and down-to-earth, creating an atmosphere of belonging.

Children who experience adversity need a champion in their lives who can help them see beyond their circumstances and cheer them on as they take control of what they can and work toward their potential. Parents commented that they loved how I interacted with their children using stern yet respectful compassionate care.

ACKNOWLEDGE

A person who feels appreciated will always do more than what is expected.

Over the years, as both a teacher and an administrator, I came to understand that there are so many students who are simply calling out to be acknowledged. Acknowledge that they may have some flaws but also acknowledge that they have the potential for greatness. Acknowledge their humanity! Most kids/students likely do not have these exact words reverberating within their cognitive thinking, but the emotion, the plea, and the desire to be great exists within them.

As a teacher, have I faced some difficult children who needed to be removed from class? Absolutely! At some point, the 80/20 principle kicks in. (I prefer to think in terms of 90/10). I could not justify spending 90% of my time on one child while the other students got 10% of my attention. There were students I removed from the classroom, but at one point throughout that day or the following, I would make it a priority to ask them, "What is going on with you?" I acknowledged their presence and belonging in my classroom. I also showed high expectations for their cooperation. By providing them with the space to explain and acknowledge their shortcomings, students could navigate that space with greater accountability. And they knew they would receive compassionate care.

You obviously want to acknowledge every child because all children desire to be acknowledged; wants someone to see they exist. And that acknowledgement needs to exhibit authenticity, understanding them as young people with emotions rather than only as students, or perhaps just the class clown.

Rather than acknowledging only the student's failures, teachers need to recognize those characteristics that are likely hidden. Acknowledge that the student may have emotions that are being shuttered by pain, eclipsed by frustration, shadowed by agony or embarrassment or fear. These experiences or emotions can overpower a student's ability to blossom and hinder the potential for greatness.

Ironically, given my experiences with violence at home, I never resorted to physical harm or violent outbursts of any kind as a student, with the exception of one reactive moment. In addition, the respect I had for adults was instilled in me as a cultural expectation, no matter what.

Regrettably, this cultural expectation was pushed to its limits during that one portentous day in eighth grade.

As I have stated, math was the one subject I enjoyed and excelled at the most. Of all the subject areas, the math lesson was where I felt worthy of exercising my voice and participation. Yet not even my enthusiasm for algorithms, word problems, and mathematical equations could excite me given the enormous weight I carried mentally from the dysfunctional environment that existed at home. Naturally, my mental state was not connected to the day's math lesson on that ominous day.

As my eighth-grade math teacher was delivering the day's lesson, I was purposely distracting the class in hopes of getting kicked out, so I did not have to engage in the lesson for fear of being called on to answer a math problem from the previous day's homework. In typical fashion, the teacher acquiesced to my scheme and kicked me out. In an effort (although pleased to be removed) to save face with classmates, I took something from his desk and threw it across the classroom as I left. Clearly this was not an acceptable way of engagement.

The next period, as I sat at my desk, my math teacher walked in, stood in front where I was seated and grabbed me by my shirt with both hands. He pulled me towards him, then slammed me against the desk. As if that wasn't enough, he followed the slamming with a slap across my face.

It was (as one can imagine) an embarrassing moment for me, given that all the other students in the class witnessed this betrayal of trust, abuse of power, lack of compassion, and unprofessionalism. As a form of defense and protective instinct, I stood up, looked the teacher right in the eye, blurted an expletive, and kicked him in the leg.

Did the other adult in the classroom intervene? Most certainly! He threw me out of class. The principal called me into his office where I explained to him what had just occurred. He asked if I had kicked the teacher (completely ignoring all the other details of my story). I admitted to doing so. No less than ten minutes later, I was on my way to the number 14 bus stop with a suspension form in hand. As for the teacher who physically struck a minor, he made his way back to his classroom, never to be disciplined for his actions.

I went home and told Mami, only to once again be rejected and ignored. I was suspended from school, suspended from empathy, and suspended emotionally.

My trust in school (what little I had) was destroyed. If the teacher in the one subject area I loved did not acknowledge my presence and afford me the care and empathy I needed for reassurance that I mattered, then why should I care about school at all?

Belonging is an important ideology all children need to feel for acknowledgement of their existence. Without it there is a disconnect from reality with profound implications on a child's social, emotional, physical, and psychological well-being. Belonging is the glue that bonds and transforms our future ambitions into reality.

AFFIRMATION

Just when the caterpillar thought her life was over,
she became a butterfly.
                                        —Howett

How many times have you encountered or come across a student who exhibits behaviors indicative of low self-esteem, social and emotional instability, isolation, and/or depression? This is not to suggest that everyone in the educational field is trained or certified to diagnose these conditions or has the capacity to intervene as one who's professionally trained. Nonetheless, as that adage goes, "It takes a village to raise a child." Consequently, we are then left with the reality that our role as teachers extends beyond the denotative construct defined by the dictionary. We are, in essence, pseudo-counselors, psychologists, and/or social workers. Using our words and actions, along with these six T.R.A.A.C.K. universal traits, we can be a child's best hope for realizing the greatness they possess through the thick shell of their cocoon façade where they may feel trapped in confusion, pain, frustration, and loneliness. Even hopelessness.

As a boy, I thought going to school (skipping school) and dealing with abuse was my life; they were the only things I knew. It was painful, mostly because there seemed to be no escape.

Like the moments I was left standing behind a screeching car or on a Chicago sidewalk, the feeling of loneliness was overwhelming. I felt no one was ever going to help me crack open that cocoon and offer that ray of hope that, "You are going to become a butterfly," and affirm there was greatness within me. Affirm that my struggles were but a historical blip. Affirm that my choices would determine my destiny, not my circumstances.

Our choices and the support from those we see as our mentors and teachers, are the influential encouragement needed to shatter the cocoon of self-doubt. This might not happen overnight but with the proper interventions and continual affirmation, hope will prevail.

CARE

When you care about somebody, you do what's best for them.
Even if it sucks for you.
—Anonymous

As I was reflecting on the word *care*, and how to best delineate its meaning in a way that encompasses the most accurate definition from the standpoint of an educator, I came across the above quote. If that doesn't underscore what educators experience daily, someone please share with me what does! It is a form of vulnerability combined with emotional selflessness; an approach to loving and caring for your students no matter what. According to Wolpow and Johnson in *The Heart of Learning and Teaching,* "Without vulnerability there cannot be love, and without mutual vulnerability and love, learning cannot be mutually transformative." In other words, as Jesse Jackson stated, "You can't teach what you don't know, and you can't lead where you won't go."

Once students experience the care and love teachers have for them as people first and as students second, your job as an educator becomes exponentially easier and may be even more personally and professionally satisfying.

Imagine the sound many of us have heard of footsteps approaching your classroom minutes after the late bell has sounded. Yes, it is that one student, Johnny! That one student who is the difference between delivering a successful lesson or testing your patience and your tolerance for disruption. It is that one student who is seeking to be removed or exercising his/her reluctance to engage in any semblance of academic learning. It is that one student who, for years, has been marginalized, chastised, suspended, socially and emotionally ignored at home and, even more consequently, by those seen as their last ray of hope.

But suppose, instead, there is a paradigm shift in our thinking about Johnny, and we treat Johnny as an asset to our classroom. Yes, you may have to put up with a few days of his nonsense (or even a few more minutes). Suppose you do not treat him with repudiation, but rather you show him that he is a smart and valued student. You ask him about his day, his life, his future. Soon, with some measure of faith, you will hear Johnny's footsteps as he comes to your class, but now he is not rushing in late to disrupt the class. Now the footsteps are rushing to your class because he knows it is the place where he will be loved and cared for. It is the place where he feels a sense of belonging. Those are no longer footsteps you hear; they are the sounds of hopefulness.

KNOW (they will succeed)

You already know something
you don't even know that you know.
—Dr. Milton Erickson

The idea of knowing versus believing, is grounded in the principle of absolutism. In other words, do you *believe* the sun is going to come up tomorrow? Or do you *know* it will rise?

When using the word *believe*, there is an element of apprehension associated with the word. If I say to Johnny, "I believe you can do this," there is that unspoken sense of uncertainty, based on Johnny's pattern of fragmented productivity, that causes a pause in our expectations for him. On the other hand, if I frame my expectations with a strong sense of self-fulfilling prophecy, "Johnny, I *know* you're going to do this," then I am telling him I have full confidence in his ability. In essence, I equip him with the space and opportunity to alter his *Looking-glass Self* (Cooley), and firmly plant the seeds of success in the mind and heart of Johnny's own self-perception.

During my tenure as principal at Bruce Guadalupe Community School, I made it a point, when addressing students who were referred to the office for disciplinary reasons, to provide some level of positive and motivational dialogue that included an "I know you can…" statement. It was a powerful way of expressing my expectations to them and sending a strong message that their success was not an option, but a reality grounded in knowing.

One example of this was a young man who found himself in my office on numerous occasions, whether for a simple violation or a more egregious one. I made it a point to always provide words of wisdom and instill in him a greater respect for responsibility, accountability, and personal growth. It was in the knowing you will succeed that years later, as an educator himself, he wrote the following words to me:

> *Thank you!!! I was your student, and you never gave up on me. I went from a troubled student to a strong teacher because of you. I owe you one!!!*

Nelson Mandela was quoted as saying, "What counts in life is not the mere fact that we have lived; it is what difference we have made to the lives of others that will determine the significance of the life we lead." The mark of successful teachers is not only defined by the quality or delivery of a lesson plan, but undeniably by the indelible mark teachers leave on the lives of their students. Although there are countless gifts we can provide our students that lead to personal growth as well as intellectual success, "self-efficacy" is at the center of all gifts. When students *believe* they belong, they respond at the moment. When they *know* they belong, they live it, creating a mindset of confidence and purpose.

The world will not only judge you by how you live your life, but how others live their lives because of you. How then can you as an educator be that difference between students believing they belong or knowing they belong?

I have a modest suggestion: T.R.A.A.C.K. all the children you come across, and be their guiding light, be their ray of hope, be their agent of change, be their answered prayer, be the love they seek, but most importantly, be the greatest teacher they have ever had! Help them navigate to the place where they can run around their diamond of life and experience their own *wow*—their reason for being—and ultimately finding their home.

I end with this simple but powerful principle:

"Love to live, so you can live to love."

LETTER TO STUDENTS AND EDUCATORS

This tenth inning, the extra inning, is deeply important and significant to me. My mother passed away on October 10, 2010. 10/10/10. Although no longer with us on earth, we know she lives on in our hearts, memory, and most importantly—heaven. So, it is with her spirit that I write and dedicate this Chapter 10 to you, the students and amazing educators!

I started this journey on January 20, 2020, Martin Luther King Day! I recall walking out for the last time the one place I had called "home" for 19 years, Bruce Guadalupe Community School, with a little uncertainty of what the future had in store for me.

Like many of us who go through transitions in life, this was my moment to acknowledge as Martin Luther King famously stated, "I have a dream." Although at that precise moment I was unsure of what that dream was, I was prepared to accept whatever God had in store for me, and use my life and professional experiences to help others navigate and realize their own aspirations and dreams to find their way home. So I end with this letter to you, the students and educators.

Dear Students and Educators:

Although the process of writing this book began during the winter of 2020, my journey around the proverbial diamond started as a young eager dream-filled adolescent well over 40 years ago. As an impoverished child, I had to overcome numerous challenges that helped construct my building blocks of perseverance. I convinced myself that this isn't the way it's supposed to be.

This mindset provided the platform for seeing the silver-lining in every storm. As an adult, I was able to direct my attention to the good of what was to come from undesirable and uncontrollable situations. Life wasn't over, just redirected. Dreams weren't broken, just redefined. Love wasn't absent, just reintroduced.

During this memoir journey, I was faced with the daunting reality that the pain and memories I thought had been erased from my mind, heart, and soul were sitting deep down in the pit of my existence. They were lurking like a lion preparing to pounce on its prey at just the right moment and that moment launched itself, for me, from the first questions my co-writer raised about the impacts of my childhood experiences. How naïve I was to think that those memories that shaped me were painless episodes, nothing more than a thing from my past to be forgotten. Was I ever wrong!

Writing about people's repressed memories, Talkspace author Jessica Dubois-Maahs states: *"Repression serves as a defense mechanism where a person unconsciously pushes away painful or traumatic thoughts and memories. It often allows a person to live a relatively normal life while being seemingly unaware of the existence of such painful experiences."*

Conversely, suppressing childhood trauma can be a voluntary act; a deliberate attempt to forget or push back painful memories. Denying the very existence of these memories can cause the increased potentiality of depression, stress, and emotional numbing.

For over 25 years, I suppressed my childhood trauma, allowing the opportunities I've had to serve as distractions, as ways to avoid delving into my past. I navigated through life as if my trauma were left behind with my adolescent years, never to be heard of or felt again for the rest of my life. I had allowed my heart to harden. I became somewhat emotionally numb. I became fearful of rejection, which is something I struggle with to this day. Despite these challenges, I continue to make strides enabling my self-confidence to govern life as it presents itself and trusting that there are many matters I can control. And I do not belabor matters that are out of my control.

What has nurtured this development? Taking advantage of opportunities presented to me has led to exciting and eye-opening events. Perhaps this willingness to seize opportunities came from Papi's allowing me to ride my motorcycle without restraint or tossing me the keys to the boat. *"El tiene que aprender.* He has got to learn," he said. Or from Mami spoiling me as a small child by showering me with kisses and simply making a special pot of rice, or whatever I requested, just for me. There are positive foundational memories amid the later traumas.

As an adult, some of the opportunities presented to me have come from good fortune; experiences I had never dreamed were possible. Others were opportunities I seized when they presented themselves. All have helped reshape my perspective.

Preparing for and playing professional baseball for the California Angels as a minor leaguer (albeit a very short time) was life-changing. It was a dream I pursued and achieved.

I have served as an extra on three different motion pictures: *Major League* (picture with Charlie Sheen), *Mr. 3000* (meeting Bernie Mac), and *Rookie of the Year*. Again, these were experiences I could not have envisioned.

I was invited to participate in the University of Wisconsin Rural Leadership Program (WRLP) that focuses on preparing leaders to address community and organizational challenges. I accepted the invitation.

As a WRLP participant, I traveled to India to learn about their educational, economic, political, and health care programs. During this visit, I witnessed poverty at unimaginable levels. I saw communities of people living in cardboard boxes, children left alone to fend for themselves, and alarming rates of hunger. Many times, other WRLP members and I broke down in tears seeing these destitute conditions. India redefined my attitude about "need" vs. "want." There is very little I need. Rather, I now use "I want" statements. We also learned about beauty in India as we visited the Taj Mahal and swam in the Indian Ocean. We welcomed the colorful decorations adorning so many cows.

One year after the devastation from Hurricane Katrina, our WRLP group traveled to New Orleans' 9th Ward. Seeing this destructive storm epicenter was sobering. There were stumps and driveways, but no houses. There were houses with symbols written on the front doors indicating the number of survivors in the home, and the number of deceased. It was heartbreaking, to say the least.

During my time at Bruce Guadalupe Community School, I also had the opportunity to visit Cuba to provide pharmaceuticals and school supplies to impoverished communities. We traveled to different segments of the country and I got to meet and shake the hand of Prime Minister Fidel Castro.

Each of these opportunities were moments I seized. I did not consciously realize I was stepping beyond adolescent traumas by softening my heart, embracing emotions, and growing my self-confidence. But I was.

Pascual with Charlie Sheen (L) and Wesley Snipes (below) in the movie *Major League*.

Mr. 3000 photo with good friend, Johnny Rodriguez.

I was preparing for joy. My most life-changing event was marrying my incredibly beautiful girlfriend, Caroline, and one year later, starting our family.

Starting a family gave me the opportunity to redefine my perception of what a family should look like and how it can function. Most importantly, I committed myself to doing things differently than what I had experienced. I was able to see fatherhood from the point of view of my children. It didn't come without its difficulties, but I was determined to change the patterns from my youth.

Following my abrupt release from the California Angels minor league team because of my injuries, and having no post-secondary educational experience, I knew education was my ticket to provide a better life for myself and my family. I enrolled in college although I knew little of what was to come from that

At the Taj Mahal, New Delhi, India. (2011)

decision. My fear of failure was more significant than my desire to quit.

There were countless times that our children went to bed and woke up without seeing their father. I missed some of my children's first steps and first words. I was (I like to refer to it as) an excused temporary absentee father. I was neither ignorant nor dismissive of the reality of our family situation, and the impacts my responsibilities of work, school, and family care had on both my wife and children. But I made the choices for unselfish reasons to improve our family position on the socioeconomic scale. It has improved our collective future and, as of today, our family has benefited ten-fold from the choices.

These collective opportunities and life changing experiences allowed me to focus my attention, for the time being, on life-improving responsibilities. My focus was an unconscious avoidance of the inner pain and memories of my childhood trauma. As fate would have it, life has a way of uncovering traumatic experiences and exposing our vulnerabilities at just the right moment.

My moment began with this book. No sooner than I began this process, the unattended wounds and scabs that plagued my heart and soul surfaced like a whale breaching its ocean home and splashing down creating a ripple effect of emotional reminiscence of deeply hidden stories of pain.

As I continued to round the bases of my long-neglected diamond, and face history with all its distressing recollections, I found myself finally home and ready to share my story with others. Especially you—the students and educators who are currently experiencing or acknowledging your own painful past—so you can come to an understanding that circumstances don't define or determine your destiny. The choices you make undoubtedly will.

I hope this book can help others become polished "diamonds in the rough" and lead them to their own re-directed lives, re-defined dreams, and re-introduction to love. This is the one true place we can all call home.

ACKNOWLEDGMENTS

This journey could not have been accomplished, let alone possible, without the support and encouragement from so many. At the heart of this journey was my loving mother's spirit, which has remained with me from the moment she took her last breath 11 years ago. Mami, I know life wasn't always kind to you, and you battled demons along the way. However, I am secure in the knowledge that your love for us never waivered, and you are now resting in eternal peace. *Te quiero tanto.*

My wife Caroline, thank you for your love, and support, and for the instrumental role you played. Truthfully, this book would not have been completed without your continued support, emotional investment, engagement, and encouragement. You are the one person who intimately knows the pain and emotional rollercoaster of my life story and how it has impacted me. You were there throughout all the laughter and tears as I uncovered deeply tucked-away memories, by providing a shoulder to cry on, an attentive ear, and unconditional love. Although this book is about my story, it's a story that couldn't be told had it not been for your intervening compassion and supportive nature.

Although we come to believe that it takes a village to raise a child, it is also true that it takes a supportive family, friends, and community to serve as mentors, life coaches, and even counselors to navigate through life's challenges. I've been fortunate to have many around my arena that serve as such. Outside of my mother and wife, my children—Pascual, Andrew, Monica, and Emilie—have given me the motivation and passion to be the best parent I could be. All I am is because of your inspirational presence in my life.

To my sisters, Alicia and Dalila, your loving support and our unbreakable bond serve as one of my greatest blessings. Our vulnerable childhood stories, coupled with the successes we have gained thus far, prove that we are survivors. We unconsciously discovered that life is not defined by our circumstances, but by the choices we make. I love you both dearly.

To all my friends and professional colleagues who served as pillars of support, in particular, Rafael Acevedo and the Acevedo family, Sebio and Mani Rodriguez, Elvis and Jessica Alverado, Dr. Juan and Blanca Baez, Virgillio Rodriguez, Brenda Rodriguez, Luz Carby-Ortiz, Dora Acosta, Dr. Walter Sava, Wilma Bonaparte, both Fr. Rick Abert and Fr. Mike Bertram, Dr. Joanna Ruth-Love and countless others, I thank you for allowing me to be a part of your story, as you are a significant part of mine.

A special thank you to four individuals who played a meaningful role in the development of this book: Dr. Juan Baez, Christin Johnson, Rebeca Clement, and Dr. Gabriel Velez. And of course, my thanks to Judith Gwinn Adrian, my co-writer who played an instrumental part in this book's development. And to my publisher, Kira Henschel, HenschelHAUS, Milwaukee, for her patient and understanding guidance. Thanks, Kira!

ACKNOWLEDGMENTS

The following four gracious individuals provided meaningful feedback that in all honesty, has enhanced this book for the readers enjoyment. Their input was insightful, enlightening, and educational. I will forever be grateful for their time, support, and generosity for taking time to share in this experience with me. They are no longer simply friends, but fully embedded as family members of the Rodriguez family.

Dr. Juan A. Báez currently serves as the principal at Milwaukee School of Languages in Milwaukee Public Schools. He has been an MPS employee for 20 years.

He began his career as a 6th-grade bilingual teacher at Kosciuszko Middle School. He has also served as an assistant principal at U.S. Grant School, and later as principal of Hopkins-Lloyd Community School, and then Alexander Mitchell Integrated Arts School. In his most recent role, he served as Co-Director for the Department of Black and Latino Male Achievement MPS. He graduated from the University of Wisconsin–Madison with a bachelor's degree in history. He earned both a master's degree and doctorate in educational leadership at National-Louis University.

Dr. Báez was born in Rio Piedras, Puerto Rico, but was raised in Milwaukee. He attended Vieau School and graduated from North Division High School. Dr. Báez believes that educators are the pillars of change in our communities and that education is the great equalizer for our children. Dr. Báez's philosophy is that all children are capable of amazing achievements when they receive the right opportunities.

Christin Johnson is a school counselor with nearly 20 years of experience in education. Christin has devoted her professional life to advocating for students and best preparing them for academic and social-emotional success in kindergarten through 12th grade, college, and beyond. Christin earned a master's degree from UW-Stout in School Counseling in 2003, and graduated from Carroll University in 2001 with a double major in communication and Spanish. Christin resides in Port Washington, WI, with her husband, two daughters, and golden retriever, where they enjoy outdoor activities as a family during all seasons. Now a middle school counselor at Thomas Jefferson Middle School in Port Washington, Christin previously worked for the United Community Center in Milwaukee, WI. There she served both as an elementary and middle school counselor for the agency's K-8 public charter school, Bruce Guadalupe Community School. During her tenure with the United Community Center, Christin also served as the Director of UCC's Pre-College Program, collaborated with Greater Milwaukee-area organizations and universities to develop unique college and career exploration opportunities for first generation college students, and introduced school-centered mental health programming for Bruce Guadalupe students and families.

Rebecca Reyes-Clement is currently an elementary special education teacher but has also served as an early childhood special education teacher, an instructional coach, regular education teacher, and paraprofessional since beginning her teaching career in Milwaukee in 1999. Rebecca grew up on the near South Side of Milwaukee and is committed to serving youth in her home community. She continues to live in the Milwaukee area with her husband, son, and daughter.

Rebecca graduated from the University of Wisconsin-Milwaukee where she earned her early childhood special education license. She also has her undergraduate degree in psychology from Upper Iowa University and an associate degree in human services from Milwaukee Area Technical College. She is currently pursuing a dual master's in Curriculum and Instruction and Administration from Alverno College.

Her teaching philosophy is inspired by the quote by Ignacio Estrada: "If a child can't learn the way we teach, maybe we should teach the way they learn."

Dr. Gabriel Velez is an assistant professor and developmental psychologist in the Department of Educational Policy and Leadership (EDPL) in the College of Education at Marquette University. Dr. Velez studies identity development in adolescents, particularly in relation to civic development, human rights, and peace, including young people's understandings and responses to peace education and restorative practices in their schools. He has collaborated extensively with schools and nonprofit educational organizations in Milwaukee and Colombia. He received a BA in history and literature from Harvard University, and an MA and PhD from the University of Chicago in comparative human development. A detailed listing of his work can be found at https://marquette.academia.edu/GabrielVelez, and he can also be followed on Twitter at @GabrielMVelez or contacted via email at gabriel.velez@marquette.edu.

Lastly, to you, the reader, I thank you for reading this book with an open mind and for allowing my experience as a child, adolescent, adult, and professional to enter into your heart and consciousness, while inviting the written words to permeate your soul and invite your own experiences to guide you to your why and eventual home. May God bless each and everyone of you in your personal and professional careers.

APPENDIX
ADVERSE CHILDHOOD EXPERIENCES
(ACE)

Here are the ACE assessment questions. The number of "yes" answers equates to your ACE score.

Prior to your 18th birthday:

Did a parent or other adult in the household often or very often… Swear at you, insult you, put you down, or humiliate you? or act in a way that made you afraid that you might be physically hurt? No___If Yes, enter 1 __

Did a parent or other adult in the household often or very often… Push, grab, slap, or throw something at you? or Ever hit you so hard that you had marks or were injured? No___If Yes, enter 1 __

Did an adult or person at least 5 years older than you ever… Touch or fondle you or have you touch their body in a sexual way? or Attempt or actually have oral, anal, or vaginal intercourse with you? No___If Yes, enter 1 __

Did you often or very often feel that … No one in your family loved you or thought you were important or special? or Your family didn't look out for each other, feel close to each other, or support each other? No___If Yes, enter 1 __

Did you often or very often feel that … You didn't have enough to eat, had to wear dirty clothes, and had no one to protect you? or Your parents were too drunk or high to take care of you or take you to the doctor if you needed it? No___If Yes, enter 1 __

Were your parents ever separated or divorced? No___If Yes, enter 1 __

Was your mother or stepmother… Often or very often pushed, grabbed, slapped, or had something thrown at her? or Sometimes, often, or very often kicked, bitten, hit with a fist, or hit with something hard? or Ever repeatedly hit over at least a few minutes or threatened with a gun or knife? No___If Yes, enter 1 __

Did you live with anyone who was a problem drinker or alcoholic, or who used street drugs? No___If Yes, enter 1 __

Was a household member depressed or mentally ill, or did a household member attempt suicide?

No___If Yes, enter 1 __

Did a household member go to prison? No___If Yes, enter 1 __

ACE scores of 4 or more on a scale of 1-10 show a 240% likelihood of depression and 1,220% likelihood of suicide. Having an ACE score of six would indicate significant challenges to being successful (being well in mind, body, and spirit).

There are ten types of childhood trauma measured in the ACE Study. Five are personal: physical abuse, verbal abuse, sexual abuse, physical neglect, and emotional neglect. Five are related to other family members: a parent who's an alcoholic, a mother who's a victim of domestic violence, a family member in jail, a family member diagnosed with a mental illness, and the disappearance of a parent through divorce, death, or abandonment. Each type of trauma counts as one. So a person who's been physically abused, with one alcoholic parent, and a mother who was beaten up has an ACE score of three.
https://www.acesconnection.com/blog/got-your-ace-resilience-scoresacestoohigh.com/

BIBLIOGRAPHY

Ali, M. (1996). Cited in T. Hauser, *Muhammad Ali: In Perspective* (p. 175). New York: HarperCollins.

Braman, L. (2021). https://lindsaybraman.com/positive-childhood-experiences-aces/

Churchill, W. Quoted in *Change Catalysts* (2016). https://www.changecatalysts.com/what-can-winston-churchill-teach-us-about-leading-change/

Cooley, C. H. (1902). *Human Nature and the Social Order*. New York: Scribner's.

Cooley, C. H. (1902). *Looking-glass self. The production of reality: Essays and readings on social interaction.* New York: Scribner's.

Drevitch, G. (2021). *How Identity Change Happens.* https://www.psychologytoday.com/us/blog/finding-new-home/202107/how-identity-change-happens

Dubois-Maahs, J. (2019). Retrieved from The Talkspace Voice: https://www.talkspace.com/blog/why-we-repress-memories/

Erickson, M. https://www.coolfunnyquotes.com/author/dr-milton-erickson/already-know/

Mandella, N. quoted in Dana Forde, (2014). Mandela's life inspires service community https://www.nelsonmandela.org/news/entry/mandelas-life-inspires-service-community

Howett, B. H. (2007). *Ladies of the Borobudur.* Denver: Outskirts Press, Inc.

Jackson, J. (1987). *Straight From the Heart.* Philadelphia: Fortress Press.

King, M. L. (1968). Washington D.C. address. Retrieved from https://www.goodreads.com/quotes/37292-we-must-accept-finite-disappointment-but-never-lose-infinite-hope

Maxwell, J. (2013). Retrieved from *Finding My Purpose*: https://www.youtube.com/watch?v=0Qr_vJvqItY

Melvin, *Harold and the Blue Notes, Wake Up Everybody* (2011). https://www.youtube.com/watch?v=-TDfPgd3Kyc

Nishah, H. (n.d.). http://thoughtsofasimplecitizen.blogspot.com/2014/12/book-review-tao-te-ching.html

Office of Civil Rights, U.S. Department of Education (2018). *School Climate and Safety*. Washington, D.C.: United States Department of Education.

Oxford English Dictionary (2018). OED online, www.oed.com

Rohn, J. (n.d.). Quoted in https://www.goodreads.com/quotes/561636-your-life-does-not-get-better-by-chance-it-gets

Sapolsky, R. M. (2018). "The teenage brain: Why some years are (a lot) crazier than others." https://bigthink.com/videos/what-age-is-brain-fully-developed

Scott, M. (2017). *Even on Your Worst Day, You Can Be A Student's Best Hope*. Alexandria: ASCD.

Tzu, L. (6th Century BC). *Tao Te Ching*. Chapter 23.

Wenz, M. (2019). *Flipping Your Lid—The Effects of Trauma on a Child's Brain*. https://familyandchildtherapy.com/2019/10/07/flipping-your-lid-the-effects-of-trauma-on-a-child's-brain/

Wolpow, R., & Mona M. Johnson, R. H. (2016). *The Heart of Learning and Teaching: Compassion, Resiliency, and Academic Success*. Washington: Washington State Office of Superintendent of Public Instruction (OSPI) Compassionate Schools.

Womak, Leeann. *I hope you dance* (2018). https://www.youtube.com/watch?v=ozR3XL4cab0

A BIT MORE INFORMATION
& PHOTO GALLERY

T he Puerto Rican community consists of many traditions, along with a variety of delectable dishes brought over from the island. The aroma of *arroz con pollo, habichuelas, pasteles,* and *pernil* are only some examples of dishes made in traditional Puerto Rican households, especially during the holidays. In addition, the art of music and dance, particularly salsa, is a gift passed down from generation to generation.

Unfortunately, there are other traditions or beliefs that rode the coattails of immigration as well. These kinds of other-worldly beliefs were real for my grandparents but somewhat less for my parents, although they too grew up in Puerto Rico. Still, the traditions lingered.

One of these beliefs is the practice of witchcraft.

This is a 1978 photo of my grandmother and grandfather sitting on a couch in their home. It speaks directly to this belief.

Maternal grandparents, Angel and Amelia Diaz (1978).

139

Neither of them is smiling in the photo. This photo is a strange portrait. My grandmother was very superstitious about people taking her picture. In Puerto Rico, as a young girl, she had been taught that people would use photos to do *brujeria,* witchcraft. The photo was taken over their protests. That wasn't surprising for my grandfather, who was a grumpy old man. My grandmother, on the other hand, loved life, but more importantly, loved helping others, even if it meant putting her needs on pause. She was a true servant of God, living the life of a true, altruistic humanitarian.

Paternal grandparents
Hipolito and Cecilia Rodriquez.

MY BELOVED FAMILY

Caroline and Pascual celebrating their 25th anniversary in Hawaii (2016).

From L to R: Pascual Jr., Monica, Pascual Sr., Caroline, Emilie, and Andrew.

Pascual Jr. and Colleen Rodriguez celebrating their wedding day– August 28, 2021.

Milwaukee Business Journal, 40 Under 40 Award, 2003.

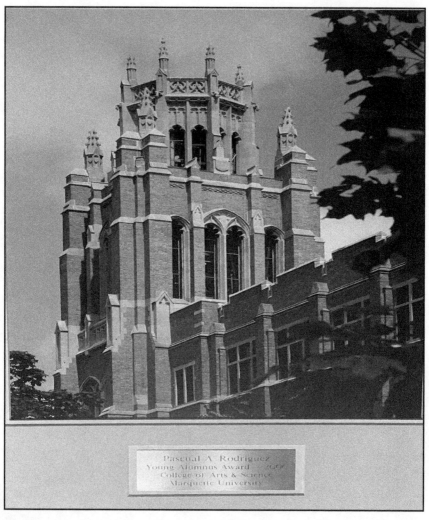

2007 Young Alumni of the year award from Marquette University.

ABOUT THE AUTHORS

Pascual A. Rodriguez has a master's degree in School Leadership and Administration from National Louis University and an undergraduate degree in secondary education from Marquette University. Pascual's journey in writing the memoir began in January of 2020. With more than 25 years of educational experience, Pascual has served as a teacher at Bay View High School (MPS) and for most of his career served as principal at Bruce Guadalupe Community School (19 years). He is currently the executive principal at La Casa de Esperanza charter school in Waukesha. More information about Pascual, this book, and speaking engagements is available at www.Muevete1010.com.

Judith Gwinn Adrian, co-author. Judith has a Ph.D. in adult learning from the University of Wisconsin—Madison Pascual and Judith became a team, organizing and writing his memoir, mostly via Zoom meetings during the Covid-19 pandemic. A shared adventure. After retiring from 25 years of teaching at Edgewood College in Madison, Adrian has written and/or co-written ten books. Each of the books has been its own journey of shared memories and storytelling. Please visit www.judithadrian.com for more information.